The Library of Pastoral Care

The Library of Pastoral Care

TITLES ALREADY PUBLISHED

Sick Call: A Book on the Pastoral Care of the Physically Ill
Kenneth Child

Caring for the Elderly
H. P. Steer

The Pastoral Care of the Dying
Norman Autton

The Pastoral Care of the Bereaved
Norman Autton

Casework and Pastoral Care
Jean Heywood

Marriage Preparation
Martin Parsons

Principles of Pastoral Counselling
R. S. Lee

Pastoral Care in Hospitals
Norman Autton

Marriage Counselling
Kenneth Preston

IN PREPARATION

The Pastoral Care of Adolescents
Michael Hare Duke

Retreats
W. R. Derry (editor)

In his own Parish: Pastoral Care in Parochial Visiting
Kenneth Child

The Pastoral Care of the Mentally Ill
(Revised edition)
Norman Autton

Other volumes are planned

Library of Pastoral Care

MARRIAGE COUNSELLING

Marriage Counselling

KENNETH PRESTON

LONDON
S·P·C·K
1968

First published in 1969
by S.P.C.K.
Holy Trinity Church
Marylebone Road
London N.W.1

Made and printed in Great Britain by
William Clowes and Sons, Limited
London and Beccles

PUBLISHER'S NOTE

The purpose of the *Library of Pastoral Care* is to help those with pastoral responsibilities to understand and exercise their function better. We believe that Mr Preston's book will do this, but we are not necessarily committed to all his opinions.

SBN: 281 02294 1

Contents

Contents

Introduction

It is clearly impossible for a book of forty thousand words to be an exhaustive treatise on Marriage Counselling. What I have tried to do is to survey the field as comprehensively as possible, and to open a few windows on that field for the apprentice counsellor to see where he should be looking, what he should be looking at, and the things he should be learning about.

While I have been writing this book I have been conscious all the time of how much I owe to others. The words of Paul to the Corinthians have been ringing in my ears: "What do you possess that was not given you?" The answer as far as this book goes is, "Nothing". If any of my friends read it I can imagine one saying, "He learnt that from me" and another "I taught him that". Everyone will see how much I owe to Dr Frank Lake and friends in the Clinical Theology Movement; Chapter 6 is based entirely upon what I have learnt from Richard Hauser; and I must pay tribute to all the wisdom, knowledge, and understanding that I have gained from my contact with Dr Margaret Cameron and other friends in the Bristol Marriage and Family Guidance Council, to Dr Alan Heaton-Ward and to Dr Alan Otlet. This distillation of all that I have received from them and the setting down of how I have put it into practice in the course of my everyday ministry as a parish priest is an expression of my gratitude to them.

I was much struck by a remark of Dr Anthony Bashford: "It is usually easier to talk about what a thing is not than about what it is, and a discussion on the theology of marriage frequently and rapidly becomes an argument about the laws of divorce." I have discussed divorce in Chapter 7, groping after some solution to the intolerable dilemma of the parish priest who, on the one hand, is aware of the traditional teaching of the Church on the indissolubility of marriage and, on the other, desires to show all the pastoral care and give all the help he can to those who have suffered a marriage breakdown and who want the support of a relationship in marriage with a new partner. I hope some readers will think I have been able to find an answer to the pastoral problem while being entirely loyal to the teaching of Christ as we have it in Mark 10 and 1 Cor. 7.10–11.

I am aware that in Chapter 6 there is more "ideal" than "practice" but I am convinced that those of us who are concerned with counselling should be equally concerned with the prevention of marital distress and be ready to consider new approaches, methods, and ideas in this field.

I was asked recently by a young priest how he could become trained in counselling. The answer is not easy to give. I am not certain how much training there is in the theological colleges. In any case such training must be limited by the lack of opportunity of experience in counselling. The colleges could give to the students a sound grounding in the principles of counselling and some knowledge of the common causes of marriage breakdown. The newly-ordained clergyman would then have some background for his work in a parish. But the best person to train a newly-ordained clergyman in counselling is his vicar, always providing the vicar is experienced in counselling himself. Sometimes when I am asked for an interview I feel able to say, "Do you mind if my curate takes part in the interview as well? If he shares the counselling with me, then he can see you when I am not available." It is not so easy to do this with marriage counselling as with other forms of counselling, and it is not easy, and perhaps not right, to say this to someone whom I have known for a long time. I find it better with someone whom I have not met before; my curate and I then begin getting to know the newcomer together.

Although in theory there may be objections to a "threesome" interview I find that in practice it works. Very seldom does anyone say he does not want a third person at the interview, and I hope I have enough respect for people's feelings to make it quite easy for anyone to refuse if he is at all diffident about the matter. One thing is certain, that the counselling does not suffer and my curate, I think, would say that he has gained enormously from the experience. As I have said, I feel more confident in suggesting the presence of a third person if I know that we are not going to be involved in marriage counselling, but the experience an apprentice counsellor gains in the general principles and practice of counselling in other matters is a good preparation for involvement in marriage counselling.

Should a clergyman offer himself as a counsellor to the Marriage Guidance Council? If he does so and is selected for training he will certainly be very well trained. In return he will be expected to spend a minimum of three hours a week in counselling at the Marriage Guidance Council centre, regularly to attend counsellors' discussions and meetings with consultants (this averages about one evening a fortnight), and to give up some time to the writing-up of notes and to correspondence. Each individual must make up his own mind as to whether he is able and willing to do this.

The apprentice counsellor must bear in mind that marriage counselling is not all success and instant miracles. Sometimes after hours of counselling with different couples we fail to see that anything worth while has been achieved. Sometimes we notice only a slight change in a situation, perhaps only a long time after the counselling has finished. But when that has been said, it is worth saying also that in my experience the time spent in marriage counselling is among the most valuable and rewarding work that a parish priest does. Looking back over several years I can think of very little that could be called a waste of time, and that was only on one or two of those comparatively rare occasions when the client did not really want to be helped but wanted to give himself the uneasy

comfort and forced satisfaction that comes from pretend-
ing to himself and others that he is taking a situation
seriously.

I would like to say something about my concept of marriage; it is a much higher one than ever appears in the book.
In writing about marriage counselling naturally I am concerned with stress and distress, difficulties and problems, the
things that lead to breakdown. A good marriage is much more
than the absence of these. A good marriage is an opportunity
for reaching a quality of personal relationship higher than
that possible in any other relationship. It is more difficult
because it is closer, more intimate, lasts longer, and because
every aspect of the human being is involved. This is not so in
even the closest of friendships. The marriage relationship
goes on in this close sense for life. Here it differs from the
parent/child relationship. This latter should become pro-
gressively less close, as the child becomes independent of the
parent and embarks on marriage himself; whereas the marriage relationship becomes closer as time goes on. The partners live under one roof for a lifetime. Theirs is a
companionship which goes on day after day, and their relationship, unless it is going to become boring, must grow
all the time. And therefore it has exciting possibilities for
always.

If marriage is a growing thing, the partners are continually
reaching a deeper understanding of each other and—through
each other—of themselves, and thus of all other human beings.
Because it is growing and vital even the happiest of marriages
will have its storms, but all the time love and companionship
and understanding are developing. A marriage may be the
supreme thing in life for those who are called to it. This is not
to say that work, friends, recreation, and other things that go
to make up living are not important; a marriage will be a
better marriage if both partners are living a full life and are
not too much wrapped up in each other.

If personality can only grow and express itself in terms of
human relationship, in a good marriage there ought to be

deeper and wider opportunities for growth and expression. This would mean that the partners would have some part of their marriage that they would share with others and some part that would be theirs and theirs alone.

It is a great truth that is hidden here (Eph. 5.32 N.E.B.)

1

Some Principles of Counselling

There are certain principles of counselling which apply to all
pastoral counselling and not only to marriage counselling.
Some of them are so obvious and so much "things that every
pastor and counsellor knows", that it would seem an im-
pertinence to put them down here. Yet in practice I find myself so often forgetting them, ignoring them, and trying to
short-circuit them, through tiredness, haste, or downright
self-centredness, that it seems worth while setting them out as
a reminder of some of the principles we work by. For the more
we are mindful of them, by that much we shall be the better
counsellors.

People are Individuals

Of course people are individuals, and this means that we
must be on our guard against being storehouses of general
remedies for general complaints. This is what we are all too
eager to be. For, pressed for time as most counsellors are, it
shortens the interview or series of interviews if we can diagnose the trouble quickly—to say nothing of jumping to conclusions on insufficient and half-digested information—and
apply a "general remedy" without any real regard to the
personalities and circumstances of the individuals involved.
What is causing frigidity in Mrs A is not the same thing that
is causing frigidity in Mrs B, and even if it were the circumstances of the two women are so different that the best way of
helping the one will be altogether different from the best way
of helping the other.

Because people are individuals they are not "cases". It is at this point that I find it necessary to keep a close watch upon myself. At the present time it is altogether too easy to talk of people as "cases". Everyone does it and although this may pass with people unknown to us personally—as for example at a "case discussion" (though even here it is not a wholly satisfactory way of thinking and talking about human beings) —with people we know as individuals it is not good. If ever I catch myself thinking of someone as a "case" I recognize that I am by that much a "case" myself. For thinking of people as "cases" is a way of keeping them at a distance. To think of them as individual human beings is to make contact and to be contacted, to be involved and committed in some measure to a personal relationship. It is to avoid the stress of personal relationships and involvement that we keep people at a distance by thinking of them as cases in our file. The modern way of speaking of "cases" is not just jargon—it is an escape mechanism.

To appreciate and understand the individuality of people it is necessary to be sensitive to them. Some pastors have by natural endowment a great degree of sensitivity, others seem to have precious little of it. The latter are to be found in every group of people; being a clergyman, doctor, teacher, social or any other kind of worker is no guarantee that one has even a modicum of sensitivity to the reactions and needs of others. Our own feelings about this are no guide at all. If we feel that by nature (or grace, if we prefer it that way) we have sensitivity or insight, then it is highly likely that in fact we are particularly obtuse and insensitive in our relations with other people, and this fact is disguised only from ourselves, an adoring wife, and one or two sycophantic parishioners. The latter are particularly unhelpful, and fulsome praise must never be taken as any sort of indication of our ability to see into the needs of another human spirit. The only safe starting point is the realization that as pastors and counsellors we need to be sensitive to the reactions of other people and that this sensitivity can be, and indeed, must be learnt, acquired, and developed. With whatever natural gift, or lack of it, we start, we must embark on the slow process of learning to be aware of what is going on inside another human being. Any progress we may make brings with it the terrifying vision of just how ham-fisted we have been in our dealings with people in the past. But sensitivity is not so much a virtue that some are born with and some are not and there the matter ends; it is an accomplishment which can be learnt and acquired, and this can encourage those of us who realize how much we have to learn in this field, to make a beginning and to go on learning.

At this point it might be asked how it is possible to learn to be sensitive. Trying to be aware of others sounds easy, but in fact it never is. It involves noticing their reactions and being concerned about them, trying to think of them imaginatively. It means remembering that how we think they should react is no real guide to what is going on inside them, and remembering that it is still less of a guide to think how we or "any ordinary person" would react. We have to try to get inside them, to feel as they feel, and to see from their point of view. Listening to other people is an important part of understanding them, but more of that later. It is useful occasionally to look at our relations with other people. If we find that things are often "going wrong", if people are upset by a word or deed that "we didn't mean to be understood like that", then it is possible that we are not as sensitive to other people as we suppose. On the other hand, if none of these things happen there is no cause for complacency. It may be that we are so insensitive that we are not making any living contact with anyone.

In taking into account the fact that people are individuals we must remember that counsellors are individuals too. We can learn much from books and from other counsellors, but it all has to become part of us and adapted to our own needs as counsellors. We shall have our own way of communicating which is ours, and ours alone; our own way of helping, our own way of ministering. More important, we shall each have our own fears, anxieties, and problems in our relationships with other people who have come to us for help. Make no mistake about it, a relationship of some sort will be established between us. It may be a warm one or a cold one, a close or distant one, a good or poor one, but relationship there will be. I can almost hear counsellors in a body crying out at this point, "It is wrong to get emotionally involved", and so it is in those terms. But in other terms every personal relationship involves our emotional life in some way. The people who come to us will talk to us and, we hope, unburden themselves to us. What they say is bound to touch us at some point, to stir hidden depths of our own beings, to make us anxious on our own account. We may not be conscious of this. But we must be aware of the fact that counsellors themselves react in all manner of ways because some of their own nerve centres are being touched. We decide that someone does not really want to be helped and we terminate the interview; we suggest a particular course of action or we fail to suggest another; we become impatient or inordinately sympathetic; we come too close to someone or severely keep our distance; we become ardently persuasive or passionately non-directive. We shall, of course, produce for ourselves and for any others concerned (our fellow counsellors, for example), excellent reasons for saying or doing what we have just said or done. The hidden truth is that we have reacted to the stirring of some spring of emotion in ourselves. Blessed is the counsellor who realizes that these things can happen. Still more blessed is the counsellor who knows himself well enough to know when they are happening to him.

It may be said that if this is the position it is better to refrain from being a counsellor. Anyone feeling this (and the best counsellors are bound to do so at times), can contemplate the words of Chesterton that if a thing is worth doing it is worth doing badly. A man may not be a very good counsellor but he is in point of fact the person to whom someone has come. He may not be the best but he is the best available. He will be lucky if he is not the only one available. Moreover, we must remember that a good deal of counselling of one kind or another is going on all the time. The man at the works who says lightly, "Well, if it were my wife, I wouldn't stand for it", or the woman in the office who says, "If it were my husband, I would leave him", is giving marriage counsel. Neither the giver of such counsel nor its recipient may think of it as such, but marriage counsel it is, and usually very bad counsel into the bargain. Anyone who goes to the trouble of reading this or any similar book is likely to be able to do better than that.

Listening

In any interview listening is by far the most important thing that we do. It is difficult for the young counsellor to grasp this. We think that people come to us for advice, and perhaps they do; we imagine that they will go away disappointed if we do not come forward fairly quickly with penetrating insight here, or life saving advice and words of wisdom there. We must understand from the beginning that we shall do much more good by listening than by anything else. People may or may not come to us for advice. They certainly will come to us because they think we will listen to them. They will just as certainly go away disappointed if we fail to listen. If a counsellor is a good listener, even if he says next to nothing positive, hardly anyone will go away from a first interview without feeling really helped.

For listening is of itself therapeutic. A common complaint nowadays is that there is "no one to listen to you". The doctor's list is so full that he has no time for prolonged listening. The same thing applies to the whole range of social workers. The clergy are, alas, not usually known for the quality of their listening powers. We think of ourselves as profferers of advice. Yet the clergy can, if they will, make time to become good listeners, for they still have some control over their use of time.

The feeling that "There is no one to listen to you" arises

not only, nor indeed principally, from the fact that the professional counsellors, of whatever kind, cannot or do not make time to listen. It arises from the experience that "There's no one interested in listening to you" in daily life. Listening is not a noted characteristic of personal relationships at the present time. Yet it makes for a man's well-being to be listened to.

A woman once came to me with what at first sight seemed to be a simple social problem, but after a number of questions and answers, the much deeper problem was uncovered of her relationship with her husband. It appeared that, although they got on reasonably well together, they never managed to communicate much to each other. In this instance, as so often happens, it was not possible for me to talk with the husband. The wife did not want me to because she thought it might embarrass him—he was "a very reserved man". But I did see the wife for an hour or so each week for six weeks. At the end of that time she came and said she felt very much better. Now I do not recall doing much for her except listen to her, ask her some questions so that I could understand her and her problems better, and express interest in her. The fact that someone was prepared to give up time to listening to her, show interest in her, understand her and perhaps try to be helpful proved to be a "ministry of healing". It was probably the first time for years that anyone had done this for her. She experienced a feeling of release and because of this could be a little more relaxed with her husband and could manage to make a little more contact with him. He in his turn found this a releasing experience for him and in some measure, although only in a small one, could respond. It would be unreal to pretend that the marriage is now near to being perfect, but the situation between husband and wife is more relaxed, the tension eased, and the relationship improved. And I did little except listen.

Asking questions is an important accompaniment to listening—provided that the right questions are asked and that they are asked in the right way. For only the right questions will produce answers which help us to understand someone better and to see the situation more clearly. The right questions are those which will enable us to explore the situation thoroughly, following any leads given to us. And questions must be asked in the right way. It is worse than useless being so eager to butt in with a question that we give the impression that we are more anxious to ask another question than to listen patiently to the last answer. Some questions that we must ask go deep and touch inflamed centres of feeling—they hurt. They are intimate, personal, and delicate. We must not be afraid of asking them, nor must we *seem* to be afraid. For fear communicates itself and fear of asking soon becomes fear of answering. We are thought to be too frightened to ask because of what we might hear. We look as though we might be shocked. On the other hand, we must ask questions carefully and with some delicacy of touch and feeling. To do otherwise, to plunge in without thought or feeling, will make us seem crude, vulgar, and insensitive. Forfeiture of confidence in us is bound to be the result.

If there is any likelihood that we are dealing with more than a trivial problem and that we may need to see someone on several occasions, perhaps once a week or once a fortnight, then the taking of notes is an absolute necessity, if we have any intention of trying to be really helpful. It is amazing how much even those with an excellent memory can forget between one interview and another. It is possible to ask the same question week after week without any awareness that it has already been asked and answered. It is very disconcerting when someone looks up and says, "You always ask that, don't you?" If notes are taken, this can be avoided and it will be possible to continue the next interview from the point where the last one ended. There will be no need to spend half an hour getting back into the picture. A glance through our notes will be all that is necessary.

The taking of notes is the more necessary the more people we are seeing. No experienced counsellor, surely, would deny the possibility of getting some details mixed and asking

Mrs Smith how Janet likes school, when the name is Judith and she hasn't started yet. Although such a lapse may not be serious from our point of view, Mrs Smith is likely to feel that we are not very interested in her if we remember so little about her. It will not mean much to Mrs Smith that she is one of the many people that we are seeing. And even if she does recognize this, she will probably have been thinking deep down that we had a special interest in her and her family and will feel correspondingly disappointed. Let us face the fact that Mrs Smith has a right to feel that we are "specially" interested in her and her family, for no family is quite the same as any other family and our relationship with a family is in that sense "special" to that one family. It is a pity if that is really so with us but we fail to convey it. The taking of notes will help us to do so.

It may be objected that taking notes will make the sessions too "clinical", too professional, and that it will destroy the easy, friendly relationship that we like to make with people. After all, it might be said, "You don't take notes when a friend comes to have tea." True. But I would certainly take notes if a friend came with a problem that needed careful investigation and he disclosed a good deal of information about himself and his situation with which I was not familiar. I have never known anyone object when I have produced pad and pen, and have said, "Do you mind if I make some notes? I find it helpful because I see a number of people and if I make notes I can remember them so much better. Also, I can read the notes I have made and see the picture as a whole, which it is difficult to do when we are talking like this, isn't it? I shall keep these notes under lock and key and no one will see them except me. When I have finished with them they can be destroyed." So far from anyone minding, people seem to be encouraged if we take notes. After all, they are used to the doctor, the social worker, the lawyer, and others taking notes, and if we do the same we give the impression that we are taking matters seriously and acting in a professional and competent manner and not just being dabbling do-gooders.

In practice I do not always make notes during the first interview. When someone comes to the door or has asked for an appointment we do not know why they want to see us. It may not be about a serious problem at all. In the first interview I am finding out why they have come and whether this is the kind of thing that is going to mean a series of interviews or something that can be dealt with in one or two at the most. After all, we do not want to engage in note taking if all that our visitor wants is to ask if we can recommend a reliable garage! When I have decided that notes are necessary I then ask if I can take them, and also add, "I think we must now start again at the beginning. Last time you were telling me something about your problem. I can now see that I may need to see you several times, if that is all right with you. So if you don't mind I'll make a few notes of the things you have told me already so that I don't forget them. Let me see, you said that . . ." I may begin taking notes some time during the first interview, often not until the beginning of the second, and there may be occasions when it is necessary to postpone the taking of notes until later still. For instance, I remember a man coming to see me who was so shy and reserved that the first two or three interviews had to be spent in gaining his confidence, and only when I considered that he felt able to trust me did I produce a notebook. But this is exceptional.

Establishing Confidence

The need to establish confidence should be self-evident. We must get people to have confidence in us and to trust us, for until they do we shall be unable to do anything worthwhile with them. When someone trusts us, then we can begin gently to feed back to him some of the insight we may have gained into his situation. This "feed-back" may be painful to him, it may be insight which he wants to resist. If he has little confidence in us we can be quite sure that he is going to be thoroughly resistant and that we shall spoil everything if we proceed. If he has learnt to trust us, then the situation is much more hopeful. Therefore, the first thing we must do is to establish confidence.

With some this is much more difficult to do than with others. Sometimes we have to spend several interviews gradually building up confidence. The simple fact of keeping appointments is one of the things that helps us to do this. Occasionally, because of a call upon our time which is over-riding, we have to change an appointment, and providing that this happens only occasionally, we can do so without forfeiting confidence. But if we are continually changing appointments and putting people off, then, whatever the reason, we shall find confidence in us becoming decidedly thin. We must be careful about how we make appointments and how we keep them. Again, listening with attention, with the whole and not with part of our minds, helps us to build up confidence. When someone is talking endlessly, pouring out a mass of trivial and irrelevant details, it is tempting to give only a part of one's mind to listening. This is soon noticed and conveys itself as unconcern. Unconcern destroys confidence.

We must never be in a hurry. Hurry is the death of confidence and good counselling. We all know the man of whom people say that he is "always in a hurry", who "is very busy" and who "never has any time". People are unlikely to come to him for counselling because he has successfully communicated the fact that he has no time for them, that he is too busy to be able to help them. But if, despite this, someone does come to him, his restlessness and obvious desire to get done and to get on with something else will rapidly destroy whatever shreds of confidence anyone may have had in coming in the first place.

There are occasions when we are bound to feel in a hurry. We have made an appointment in good faith but afterwards something has happened which makes us want to terminate the interview as soon as we reasonably can. When we are

feeling impatient and in a hurry, the important thing to remember is that we must calm down and determine that we
are not going to let anyone see the turmoil inside us. It is
essential that when we begin the interview we start as though
we have all the time in the world, are pleased to see whoever
has come to us, and have plenty of leisure to spend on them.
If an interview is begun like this, it is remarkable how after
quite a short time it is possible to say in an unhurried
manner, "Look, something has come along which means that
I can't spend as much time with you today as I usually like to.
I wonder if you would mind coming back on . . ." If the interview has begun with all the appearance of leisure, then this
will cause no distress, especially if a good relationship has
been built up by well kept appointments and devotion of
time.

It happens frequently that someone with a problem turns
up on the doorstep unexpectedly just as we are on the point
of going out and cannot possibly stay. What are we to do in a
case like this? The same principle holds good. Whatever we
feel, we must not convey haste and agitation. If we have
literally five minutes, we can ask our visitor to come in, again
in an apparently leisurely manner, let him tell us why he
wants to see us—his opening remarks will do—and say quite
unhurriedly, "I have to go out now because . . . Can you come
and see me at . . ." It is good to offer an appointment on the
same day, even if it means beginning late at night. To say to
someone, "I'm booked up all today until after 10.30; would
you like to come and see me then?" gives the impression that
we are at any rate concerned and are prepared to put ourselves out. A late appointment may not be accepted, but the
offer has been of value. And to see someone on the same day
may be a very necessary thing to do. Perhaps the person concerned is facing an acute crisis and ought to be seen without
delay; or perhaps he has taken a long time to reach the point
of coming to us to talk over a problem with us, and if we let
too much time pass between the coming and the talking, the

barriers of reserve may be put up again and be even more securely locked.

To be an accepting person is an essential qualification for anyone who desires to be a good counsellor. If we are not prepared to accept people as they are and as they come, then let us give up trying to be counsellors altogether. It may be objected that to accept people as they are is to run the risk of compromising with Christian principles. This may, indeed, happen with some counsellors. But it is possible for it never to happen. It is perfectly possible to be a thoroughly accepting person and at the same time to retain one's own personal integrity. I can think, as I write, of a woman who has just left her husband, taking with her their three small children and dragging them around from place to place giving them no settled home or background. She has come to me to "talk things over" and to "ask my advice". I can recognize that at this moment she really does not want "advice" but someone to whom she can pour out her misery. If I now begin to moralize and tell her what is right and wrong and what her duty is, I shall never be able to do anything with her. If I am patient, show sympathy and understanding, without taking sides, listen to the story of her marriage without being shocked, and accept her as a human being who is suffering a great deal of pain and unhappiness, then in time I may be able to help her. In time, too, I may have some glimmer of understanding of right and wrong in her case, though even then I am not going to be able to be sure. In response to her question, "Do you think I'm wrong?", I have been able to reply quite honestly, "How can I say? I don't know very much about you and I don't know your husband very well. It's difficult for me to say who is right and who is wrong, isn't it? In your heart of hearts you believe that what you are doing is right and surely that is what is important for you. What you are doing would be wrong for me, but then I am not you and I am not in your circumstances." If I say this, I have not condemned, I have not sermonized or moralized or laid down the law; I have accepted her as she is, a tortured piece of humanity, and perhaps by God's grace I shall be able to help her. And surely my answer is an honest one. I cannot see deeply into her life or her husband's at the moment. If her story is true, then it is likely that leaving him is the best thing for her to do, for her own sake and for the sake of her children. But it is only the picture as she sees it. The picture as her husband sees it will be a different one. How can I possibly judge right and wrong here? That kind of judgement I must leave to the good God who alone knows all the circumstances.

To accept people as they are is not only a practical necessity for anyone who wants to help them, it is the fundamental principle of respect for an individual human being.

Need it be said that a confidence at all times and in all circumstances must be respected? If something is told to us on the understanding that it is in confidence, or when this is not said is nevertheless implied or understood, then we are not at liberty to reveal anything we have been told to anyone at all, either directly or indirectly, without the consent of the person who has confided in us. This attitude on our part, when known, breeds confidence in us. Conversely nothing destroys confidence in us so much as the feeling that we can't be trusted not to let a word slip. We are not free to speak even when we think that by doing so we can greatly help the person who has reposed confidence in us. Normally we can obtain permission to speak quite simply: "Do you mind if I speak about this to your wife or would you prefer not?" "Can I mention this to A or would you rather I didn't?" That we do ask for permission to speak emphasizes the fact that we will not say a word without permission, and the disclosure of our attitude on the matter of confidences reinforces a person's trust in us.

2

Further Principles of Counselling

The Indirect Approach

It is important to realize, and at every interview to remember, that people do not always reveal at once the problem that has brought them to us. Sometimes it is too painful to speak about directly. Sometimes they do not know what their real problem is; all they realize is that they want to talk to someone about something. Sometimes they know within their heart of hearts the true cause of their distress, but they cannot face it, and so they transfer it to someone or something else. Anxiety and distress make people come to us, but they often begin by speaking about some other problem which may sound trivial or, on the other hand, desperately important. "I am worried about my daughter" may be quite genuinely "I am worried about my daughter" or it may be "I am worried about myself but I don't know how to begin to talk about myself because it is so painful to do so, so I'll talk about someone else, who is a problem anyhow." We may, indeed, be dealing with two problems. The teenage daughter may be a very big problem, but we may soon become aware that on this occasion the father comes to us because of his own concern about himself. If we are aware that people do approach us indirectly, then we can always have at the back of our minds the questions: "Is this really the thing that is bothering him or is it something else? Am I dealing with one problem or two? If one, which is it? Is he aware of the real reason he has come to me, or does he feel that he wants to talk to someone and is desperately hoping that I will help him find out why?"

The "presenting symptom", as it is called, may be trivial or otherwise. I remember someone coming to ask me if I could recommend a good place for a holiday, and this proved to be the beginning of a series of interviews dealing with a major personal problem. I also remember a man coming to the door and saying, "I thought I'd let you know that John won't be at church tomorrow, he has hurt his leg." I could easily have expressed my sympathy, thanked him for letting me know, and that could have been the end of it. But it is not usual for a father to take the trouble to come up to the vicarage to explain why his infant son will not be at church next day. The obvious thing to do was to wait and see if there was anything behind this. Without much prompting he went on: "I feel a bit guilty about it. He got up on the arm of my chair when I was trying to read the paper and I gave him a bit of a push and he fell off." Clearly this was what he wanted to talk about. But was it? One question led to another until eventually there emerged a marriage problem of very great severity and complexity. This, I am sure, was why he had come and this was what he wanted to talk about. It was not why his son would not be at church, nor even that he felt guilty about what he had done (though he may have wanted to get that off his chest too), but because of the misery in which he and his wife were living.

It is all too easy to deal with the presenting symptom rather than the root cause. If we are in a hurry or are tired, then we have a strong personal motive for doing so, and we must be aware of this. If we deal with the presenting symptom only, then the person concerned will for a time and on the surface feel satisfied and so shall we, but we shall not have been very good pastoral counsellors.

Assessing what someone says either spontaneously or in answer to questions is not easy. For the most part a man who comes to us will be quite sincere in his wish to speak the truth, but it is important for us to remember that he is speaking the truth as he sees it; it is the truth for him, but this may be very far from the whole picture. What he says, however, will certainly tell us something about himself and his own attitude, and part of our work will be to assess what he is saying, and interpret it to ourselves and perhaps to him and to his partner.

Directive and Non-Directive Counselling

The emphasis on non-directive counselling in recent years has had effects which have been both very good and very bad. It has been very good when the non-directive method has been used by an experienced counsellor, sensitive to the situation, who has known exactly what non-directive counselling should be; it has been disastrous when picked up as a technique by someone who has only imperfectly understood what it is.

We are being directive when we say to someone, "This is right . . . That is wrong . . . You ought to do this . . ." We are being non-directive when we simply help someone to sort out his own problem, to see it, and then to come to his own decision. This is usually a much better thing to do. It is better for a man to accept the responsibility of coming to his own decision. It is better for him if the decision is in fact his and not one that has been imposed upon him. But it is worse than useless if we are so obsessed with the notion of being non-directive that we cease to have anything positive to say at all. The best counsellors I know are all "non-directive", but this does not prevent them from being helpful, wise, and thoroughly positive. When someone says to me, as not infrequently happens, "I went to A some time ago but he didn't seem to have anything to suggest. He just said, 'Well, you must make up your own mind' ", then I know that in all likelihood that person has had the misfortune to come into contact with a counsellor who was determined to be non-directive but did not know what that meant. To use an illustration from shaking hands, there is a mean between someone grasping my hand and then twisting my arm and someone giving me a weak, flabby handshake that offers nothing. And so there is a mean between giving so much direction that a man's decision is not really his own and, on the other hand, being so frightened to say anything positive that we fail to give any help at all.

Another danger is that we can be so determined to be "directive" or "non-directive" that we become inflexibly one or the other. We all know the clergyman, for example, who sincerely believes that every parishioner who comes to him is looking for some positive, straightforward advice, that will tell him authoritatively what is right or wrong in his circumstances. We all know the clergyman who genuinely believes that he will be letting people down if he fails to provide such advice on every occasion. We recognize that such a counsellor is quite unaware of the fact that it is better for someone to come to his own conclusion and that the more it is his own the more he is likely to accept the responsibility for the decision. We all hope, of course, that the decision he comes to will be the one that we think the right one, but we must be prepared for him to decide otherwise. And not only that, we must be ready to recognize that in the end it is probably better for a man to reach what we consider to be a wrong decision, but one that is really his, than to be influenced by us into accepting grudgingly a conclusion to which deep down he does not really assent.

We can easily recognize the counsellor who is inflexibly and disastrously directive. What is not so readily recognized is that a counsellor can be just as inflexibly and obtusely non-directive and that the consequences can be equally disastrous. For sometimes a man or woman comes to us who, at that moment and for a time, desperately needs to be able to lean on someone and to shed the responsibility of decision. Perhaps at that moment he is able to do no more than to accept advice given and to accept it with relief. If we are so set on being non-directive that we are blind to that possibility, do not discern the true situation, fail to provide the strength looked for, and refuse to accept that temporary responsibility for another person's life, it is no good priding ourselves on being marvellously non-directive. We have actually been insensitive to the real need of another person and seriously handicapped by an imperfectly understood concept of counselling.

A good counsellor will in principle be non-directive but he will be flexible.[1]

Helping on all levels and on different levels

No one can solve another's problem for him. Sometimes a couple will express this to us. "We wish we had come to you before", they say, "before things had reached this pitch. We thought we ought to work things out for ourselves. We thought that only we could solve our own problem." They will often go on to say that they feel they have failed and have been weak because they have been unable to work things out for themselves and have been driven by their misery to bring in an outsider.

They need reassurance about this and encouragement to feel that it is strength and not weakness, courage and not cowardice, to go to the right kind of person for help, and that it is downright commonsense to do so. We can point out that they are right to feel that they and only they can solve their

---

[1] I am aware that some counsellors consider that we should never think in terms of "right" and "wrong" when we are counselling, but most counsellors have these words lurking somewhere in their minds, sometimes as synonyms for "wise" and "foolish". I am aware too that it is not the present fashion, as we imagine it once was, to think in terms of solutions which will be right or wrong for almost all men in almost all circumstances. My own view is that a counsellor should not be so vague that he gives the client the impression that no issues of right and wrong are involved on those occasions when most people would agree that there are. At the same time he must never try to impose his own point of view, and must have a great respect for the personality and individuality of his client. Questions of conscience do arise because they are sometimes at the root of a difficulty, but this is a different matter.

own problem and in the end that is what it must come to; but we can also explain that most couples need at some time or other to talk over their situation with somebody else, because one who stands outside can often see the situation more clearly and can help those involved in it to sort out what are the real problems they have to solve.

We shall be looking at some of the common causes of marriage breakdown in another chapter. At this point let us notice that we must be prepared to help people with all kinds of problems. We must be ready to help on all levels or one level only. If we are Christians, and therefore ministers of the gospel (whether ordained or lay), we shall want to minister the gospel to people; we shall feel that we have not really done the best for people if we do not do that. But it is not always possible and certainly not always wise to attempt it. It is worth remembering the distinction made between the word of life and the work of love. It is not always possible to minister the former; it is always possible to minister the latter. Christian counsellors will always want to minister the word of life. But they must recognize that it is an act of love and wisdom not to attempt to do so when, as is often the case, it is not the right time or occasion and the person concerned is not ready to receive it. It is something that a man has come to a clergyman for help. It is something but not everything, and whether it will in the course of time be anything more than a beginning may depend on the ability of the clergyman as a counsellor. If someone goes away saying to himself, "I come to a clergyman for help and all he can do is to thrust religion at me", we may have made a ham-fisted attempt to minister the word of life, but we have certainly not ministered the work of love—which at this stage may be the necessary preparation for the ministering of the word of life by someone else in another place and at a much later time.

It gives a meaning to our work of counselling and encourages us to go on giving time to it, if we remember that the work of love on its own and in its own right is an important, perhaps the most important part of our ministry. This means, among other things, being willing to help people on all levels or on one level only and equipping ourselves as best we may be able to do so. The clergy sometimes say, "If only people would come to us with their problems! But they don't. How can we get them to do so?" If we find ourselves saying that, then we must ask ourselves *why* people don't come to us. Is it because they don't think we can help them? Is this opinion justified? Have we equipped ourselves to help all kinds of people on all levels? The common experience of those of the clergy who have taken some pains about this is that the real problem is how to fit in the number of people who want to come to them for counselling. As good wine needs no bush so a good counsellor needs no advertisement. The word gets passed on: "He was very helpful to so and so ... Why don't you go to X, I found him very helpful." The difficulty soon changes from "Why don't people come?" to "How can I fit in those who do?"

Being prepared to help where we can and in any way we can means that at one time we shall find ourselves dealing with a deep personality problem or one of communication and adjustment, at another time with some comparatively trivial matter easy of solution. We must be prepared to help on the social welfare level, either acting as a kind of social case-worker or bringing in and co-operating with the appropriate statutory or voluntary case-worker. It may be with a housing problem that our help is sought, and we must remember the importance of at least making an attempt and giving careful thought to the matter, even though what we actually achieve may be little or nothing. Sometimes we shall be discussing a couple's budgeting, sometimes problems with in-laws, sometimes the physical side of marriage. In counselling one couple we may be dealing with only one of these things, with another couple with all of them and other things as well. One couple may find a quick and easy solution to their problem, another may take a very long time to make even a moderate success of their marriage.

It is necessary to accept the fact that a couple's or an individual's level of response will vary because they will have differing capacities of response. One will be able to assess a situation better than another, will be more capable of reflection and introspection. Intellectual ability will count for something but not for as much as we imagine. We must be content that what we have successfully attempted in one instance cannot necessarily be done in another.

Some Practical Points

Where do we interview people? In our own home? In theirs? In an office, if one is available? Counsellors differ in their answers to these questions. Some prefer what to them is the impersonal atmosphere of an office, feeling that it gives the client a sense of security to be coming to what seems like a doctor's surgery or a lawyer's consulting room where canons of speaking in confidence are understood and accepted. The client may feel that he knows where he is in such a place. Other counsellors like to see a couple in their own home. The thought here is that the couple will feel more at ease and therefore more relaxed in their own surroundings. Others are like me. I prefer to see people in my own study at home, at least for the first one or two interviews. For in his own study the counsellor is in familiar surroundings and can feel at home. As the person coming to see him about a marriage problem is bound to be feeling in varying degrees anxious, uneasy, or distressed, it helps the interview if the other party to it can feel comparatively at ease and relaxed. The counsellor can more easily do this on his home ground. In other words, one of the persons concerned in the first interview is going to feel on edge; there is no need for both to do so.

Do we see a couple together or separately? Usually circumstances will dictate the answer to this. In the majority of cases it will be one of the partners concerned who will come to see us or get into touch with us. We interview that one and ask permission to see the other. If permission is given, we do so; if it is withheld, we do not do so whatever the circumstances. Usually it is given and usually it will then be best to see the other partner separately. Sometimes it will be right to continue these separate interviews for a time, sometimes to see husband and wife together fairly quickly. We have to be guided by the circumstances.

Circumstances will also dictate how we approach the other person. Has the wife who has come to us told her husband that she was coming? If not, will she tell him that she has been? Is she frightened to tell him, and if so, does there appear to be reason for her fears? These and other similar considerations will have to be taken into account. Some counsellors, irrespective of the circumstances, make it their practice invariably to write to the other partner explaining, for example, that the man's wife has come to talk over their marriage and asking him if he would like to come too. Other counsellors like to make direct contact with the other partner either by a visit or by telephone. This latter course has certain advantages. The other partner is not left brooding, wondering what has been said about him; he is not left with time for his anxiety to mount, perhaps imagining that the counsellor has already taken sides with his wife and is going to moralize to him. Some may feel that such a direct approach is unfair and too sudden and that time should be given for a nervous or reserved partner to become used to the idea of talking to a third party. Each counsellor must be guided by what he judges the circumstances to be after talking with the one who has consulted him.

It is essential to realize that we cannot always be working in ideal conditions and must be prepared to work in the best conditions available. It is very important that we should not be bound by rules that we have made for ourselves, or by habits that we have formed, or by notions that we always proceed in such and such a way and that any other would be calamitous. On one occasion, for a variety of circumstances which it would not be right to discuss here, I wanted another counsellor with a particular knowledge and experience that I lacked to join with me in seeing a couple. The time factor and the circumstances were such that it would have meant the two of us together having an interview with the two of them, making a four party interview. I did not need to be told that this was not at all a good way of doing things; but in this instance it was the only way. The counsellor whose help I sought told me that he never worked like this, that it would make things very difficult, that it would not be a successful interview and that he really could not take part in it. Consequently, an opportunity was lost. The marriage ended disastrously. If the counsellor had been prepared to break his rules of interview, the end result might still have been the same; but it could not have been any worse, and it might have been better.

It is important that we should not take sides or seem to be taking sides. This does not mean that we remain aloof and detached and do not reach any conclusions. But we must not be "for him" or "for her"; we are "for them". We can say this, and it is usually accepted gladly. People know that if we are for one or the other, then we cannot help both. If the husband, for example, by something we say or by our attitude thinks that we have already been indoctrinated by his wife and have condemned him in advance, we shall never be able to do anything with him. As far as this marriage is concerned we might as well resign from the position of counsellor without any more ado. We can express sympathy and understanding with each but not take sides.

Speaking the truth as we see it goes a long way towards helping people to have confidence in us. To speak the truth might be thought axiomatic, but it is all too easy, in an attempt to be reassuring, to say "I'm sure everything will be all right" when we have no real grounds for saying it. We are often asked, "Do you think things will work out all right?" We should like to be encouraging and give a reassuring answer, but it is not reassuring to the client to say in some facile and superficial manner "I feel sure things will work out right" when either we feel nothing of the sort or, if we feel it, have no grounds for doing so. The client will soon see through our pretence and cease to have confidence in what we say. We should never destroy hopes, for no situation is entirely hopeless, but it is not wise to encourage hope falsely. In answer to the sort of question above we can always say, "I don't know. Things may work out, they may not. Let us see what we can do about the situation." This does not destroy hope but it does not encourage a false and easy optimism. Of course, where we can do so honestly we should give as much hope and encouragement as possible; but we should bear in mind that a baseless hope can be as destructive as despair.

3

Some Common Causes of Breakdown

Communication

Many counsellors, I think, would say that the commonest
cause of breakdown in marriage is lack of communication. I
know that at this point someone will say that lack of communication is often an effect and not a cause and that we
need to find out why one partner cannot communicate with
the other. There is a great deal of truth in this and we shall
be considering it in this chapter. At the moment let us observe that again and again the marriage counsellor feels that
the real cause of the difficulty with which he is dealing is
lack of communication between husband and wife.

The easiest illustration to take concerns sex. More often
than otherwise we find that the love-making of husband and
wife is far from satisfactory, to say the least of it, and that
this is giving rise to all kinds of frustrations and anxieties.
Very often the woman will express this by saying, "I don't
get any feelings", and the man will say, "My wife is cold."
A little questioning (it will have to be gentle, intimate questioning, and a sensitive enquiry into detail may be necessary)
will reveal to the counsellor that it is no wonder that the
woman "doesn't get any feelings" and "is cold", because her
husband has never come anywhere near making love to her
in a way that has given her any chance of responding.

For a man and a woman do differ very greatly sexually.
Everyone seems to "know" this but not everyone seems to
"realize" it and take it into account. A man is ready for
intercourse in a moment, the thought being all the prepara-

tion needed for the deed. He approaches his wife abruptly, thinking that she reacts to him as he does to her, touches her intimately before she is ready and before he has prepared her by love and tenderness for intimate caresses, and first wonders, then becomes irritated, and finally is annoyed because she does not respond with an ardour and passion that matches his own. He says she is "cold" and "doesn't love him", and she merely endures and is unable to respond, while he carries on to the end.

It is not wise, as a general principle in counselling, to begin working out who is right and who is wrong and to apportion the blame. But, in a situation such as we have described, if either is more to blame than the other it is probably the wife. If he doesn't understand his wife's reactions, if he goes at her (the words often used are "like a bull at a gate"), it is probably her "fault" because she has never made a determined and sustained effort to get herself over to him, to get him to understand her, to realize that she has an entirely different approach to love-making from his own. She has failed in communication.

A man does not know "by nature" what goes on inside a woman's mind; he is not born with a penetrating perception of a woman's emotional life. A husband can only begin to appreciate his wife's different attitudes and reactions if all the time she is trying to get him to understand her and she is endeavouring to convey her meaning to him, for it is very difficult for him to understand. She must be patient with his failures to understand and with his occasional failures to put into practice the understanding he has already acquired. For this coming to know and understand each other is not something that is done easily in a day or two, once and for all. It is no good for a wife to say, "I've explained to him and he won't understand", or for a husband to say, "I've told her and she won't listen." The sharing of minds, the entering into the depths of each other's personality, depends upon a long process of communication and perseverance in the face of failure to communicate. When the process of communication has ceased or where, as in so many instances, it has never begun, the result will be some form of marriage breakdown, whether concealed in apathy or revealed in more overt forms.

We have used sex and the approach to love-making as a simple and easily understood illustration of the differences between a man and a woman and of the need for each to persist in the attempt to communicate with the other that at last they do understand each other. In this respect what applies to sex applies to everything else that goes to make up what we call "personality". It is often said that a woman's approach to life is more "emotional" than a man's. What we mean is that it is socially acceptable for a woman to show her emotions in ways that are not permissible for a man, who must therefore stifle his emotions and push them under and out of sight, until they express themselves in ways that are not commonly thought of as emotional—in reticence, aloofness, anger, and a variety of other ways. A woman must try to get her husband to understand her "emotional" approach to life and to accept it, and the husband must try to explain himself to his wife so that she no longer only sees that he is different from herself but sees it with understanding.

Things come to mind that in themselves seem small but are not really so; things that we find coming into conversation again and again. "He never notices me . . . He treats me like a piece of furniture . . . He never notices when I put something new on . . . He never says anything when I have my hair done, except when he doesn't like it . . . He never says he loves me. The only time he takes any notice of me is when we go to bed, and then he's interested all right . . ." A man needs to realize how a woman likes to be noticed and told that she looks nice. He needs to understand that she wants continually to be told that he loves her. He needs to know how disastrous it is if he does not make any approving comment when she has her hair done or is wearing something new. But he can only come to understand his wife if she is making a great effort to get him to understand her.

We have seen the importance of communication when it

concerns the differences between men and women or, at any rate, between most men and most women. It is even more important when it concerns the difference between this man and that woman. For that woman is different from all other women, though having much in common with them, and this man is different from all other men. Can this man explain to his wife some of his most inmost feelings? Can he convey to her that he finds it painfully difficult to reveal himself, even to her: that on the surface he may be open and brash but underneath he is unbearably reserved and likes to keep his inmost feelings to himself? We shall be considering this sort of personality difficulty in a moment. At this stage let us do no more than notice the need for an effort at communication. If in five years' time, or even two, Prince Charming is saying, "My wife Cinderella doesn't really understand me", then it is probably his fault for not having made a real and continuous effort at communication. In the circumstances how can she understand him?

The marriage counsellor can do a great deal to help here by pointing out, for example, how difficulties have arisen not because they do not love each other but because of their lack of communication. This immediately relieves the pressure on the couple, for they have been thinking and dreading that the trouble is that they do not love each other. The counsellor can almost feel the atmosphere lighten and the couple saying to themselves, "So that's all it is." The counsellor will think that is quite enough! The counsellor can begin to interpret the one to the other and the process of communication can begin through him. No one who has been in the position of interpreter and has seen on the faces of those to whom he is speaking the growing awareness and realization of each other's different situation can fail to recognize the importance of the counsellor's role as interpreter. The process of communication once begun can continue, for a time, perhaps, with the help of the counsellor, and then without him. I remember counselling a husband and wife who had been married thirty years and were now in their sixties. The wife had come to see me first, and all I could do at the time was to give her a little support to make the best of the present situation; for clearly there had been no communication between husband and wife for years and he, I was told, was a very reserved man who would greatly resent it if he knew his wife had come to me. They were not living in married misery with bickering or worse, but in that hell of non-living apathy which is all the existence there is for a married couple who share the same bed and board but have no true contact with each other. Thirty years of living together with no communication is a long habit to break, but some time later the husband and wife came to see me together on an entirely different matter. One thing led to another until we were discussing some of the difficulties of married life. And then they began to communicate with each other obliquely and somewhat remotely, using me partly as an interpreter and partly as a "communications satellite". Both, I think, felt a great relief at being able to get to each other in this way and I believe that there is now some warmth in that relationship which had not been there for a very long time.

I have recently been seeing a couple whom I first met when one of them came to see me to ask what to do to obtain a separation. This, at any rate, was the initial enquiry. After a time I remember saying, "I will certainly get the information for you, if you want me to, but from what you tell me this isn't a marriage breakdown. The trouble is that you've never tried to communicate with each other and to help each other to see what is going on inside you."

An engaged couple are often told that they must try to understand each other. It is much more important that they should try to get themselves understood.

What has been said about communication should be borne in mind when we consider other causes of marriage breakdown. For whether we are considering personality problems, sex, or any of the other things that cause, or are involved in, a marriage breakdown, defect of communication is there too.

Personality problems may, for example, cause the stress; lack of communication transforms the stress into distress.

Personality Problems

It would be foolish to pretend to be able to say very much worth while about personality problems in a short section of a small book, and I shall certainly not attempt to do so here. Here we will consider in a very simple manner some of the ways in which men and women react, and observe how these reactions affect a marriage. This will do no more than introduce the apprentice counsellor to the whole field of personality problems, but that is all it can do or is intended to do.

We all, without exception, have our interior stresses and anxieties. Their origins are to be found both in genetic make-up and environmental conditioning, in other words in the nature with which we were born and in what has happened to us since birth. These inward stresses may be known to us and recognized by us but more probably they may not. Whether known or unknown they cause us to react in certain ways. First, for example, there is the man who inwardly is reserved, shy, and afraid. Outwardly he may not show it. He may mask it from all, except those who can read the signs, by a superficial geniality or the appearance of being a strong, silent man. Inwardly he is terrified of being hurt by people, and therefore is unable to be entirely open with them and commit himself in a warm relationship. If someone comes too close to him he finds the closeness first exhausting and then unbearable and must break away and detach himself until he is ready for a fresh encounter. Another side of his personality desperately desires contact. With his wife, therefore, he will be moving sometimes towards her and then in reaction away from her. She, poor woman, will not know where she is and in bitterness and in bewilderment will complain that he is "Not there", that he "shuts himself up in his own little world", that he is "not interested in anyone outside himself". At the time all this will be true, but no sooner will she have adjusted herself to the situation than he will be moving towards her again and seeking relationship. We can see the difficulties there will be in this man's marriage whatever type of personality his partner may have. But supposing he is married to a woman whose problem is one of separation, whose inward stress is such that it is an impossible strain for her to be alone or feel alone. She is driven by forces within her which she neither knows nor understands, to seek perpetual contact with her husband, and with every fibre of her being to clutch and cling to him. She is compelled to make emotional demands which he finds impossible to fulfil. It may be asked how two such people ever came to marry one another. The question here is irrelevant; the fact is that such people frequently do, and it is not difficult to see how they will destroy each other.

Then there is the man who, whether he is conscious of it or not, feels that the world is against him. He is touchy and sensitive to every imagined insult, attack, or infringement of his position. He is aggressive in order to forestall or counteract other people's imagined aggression towards him. If he can look at himself with any degree of truth and perception, he will recognize that within he feels weak, small, and insecure, while outwardly in consequence he is for ever standing up for himself and his rights.

We can see the kind of problem such a man will be to his wife and children. He will be stern and unbending and insistent on his rights as husband, father, and head of the family. Every move that does not match his mood exactly will in his eyes be a move against him.

The partner in another marriage, the wife, let us say, is a woman who cannot feel at ease unless everything is just right. She must perpetually be tidying, cleaning, and setting in order. She has her own ceremonial which she must perform meticulously to propitiate her own inner gods. The purpose of a home, one might deduce from her behaviour, is that there should be a place for her to keep spotless and in immaculate order. She makes the life of her husband and family a misery.

This is no more than a rough sketch of four different types of personality and an illustration of the basic fact that a man or woman is compelled by inward stresses to act and react in ways that are understandable (if at all) to him or her alone. But people are very complex and rarely fit into clearly defined categories. We can all of us recognize something of each type in ourselves, possibly more of one than another, but usually something of each. We know that at times we feel the effect of our inner anxieties and stresses more than at others. We know, either of ourselves or of others, that some people seem fixed in a pattern of personality that makes life particularly difficult for others. In our counselling we have to take into account the problems caused in a marriage by the inward stress of one or both of the partners. Sometimes the stress will be slight, sometimes severe, but it can seldom be disregarded by the counsellor without loss to the value of his counselling.

What can the counsellor do? First, he can acquire some knowledge of personality and some skill in recognizing the meaning of what is taking place inside a marriage. He must learn how to observe what is taking place inside each partner to a marriage. He must be able to read the outward and visible signs of the inward and invisible distress. Then he will be in the position to help each partner to see and understand the truth about himself, and to see, understand, make allowances for, and accept his partner.

What we have said about communication now becomes important. For once a husband has (with a counsellor's help) made a beginning of understanding himself, and a wife of understanding herself, and once both have seen how they react and why, they can proceed on their own, falteringly and timidly perhaps, to communicate with each other and to develop an openness and sharing of minds which before they found impossible.

Different Approaches to Marriage

Differences in approach to marriage cause breakdown if they are not resolved at an early stage. "Approach to marriage" may be defined as what a person thinks marriage is meant to be and what he or she thinks is the role of husband, wife, parent, and child. Differing points of view about marriage should ideally be talked about before marriage, but frequently they are not.

A husband, let us suppose, has grown up in a family which the man has dominated. The man has taken the decisions, his wife and family have fallen into line. The woman has had her clearly defined role in the house and with the children, for which purpose the man has made her an allowance from his wage packet, the full contents of which she may never have known. This will be the husband's view of what a marriage is and the man's role in it, and his viewpoint may be reinforced by conversations with friends who think the same. His wife on the other hand may see the marriage as a partnership.

We can multiply examples of this: a wife expecting a husband to be mature and responsible may be married to a man who is looking for a second mother, and who wants to lean, depend, and avoid responsibility; a man who thinks that a woman's place is in the home may have a wife who wants to go out and work.

Once more we see the importance of communication in a marriage, and we can see how a counsellor must be aware of the arguments and frustrations that arise because the two partners to a marriage have begun from different ideas of what marriage is and have continued to travel on parallel lines that could never meet. The counsellor can help them to see how the real difference is a difference in point of view about marriage itself; he can help them to see what this difference is; he can encourage them to share their minds and to try to develop a common point of view.

External Pressures

It is not easy to assess what part external pressures are playing in a marriage breakdown. Some people might say that the real point at issue is the relationship between husband and wife, and that if this is a very good one then it will stand up against the severest pressures of environment. Others will say that external pressures matter so much that the survival of a marriage will depend on them.

The counsellor must try to evaluate the internal relationship and the external circumstances. He must come to some conclusion as to whether in the marriage with which he is dealing the basic problem is the relationship (and the external problems are only exacerbating, and, at the same time, masking the problem), or whether the relationship is fundamentally a sound one but the external difficulties are such that any marriage would wilt under them.

External difficulties, that is difficulties external to the relationship, include inadequate housing, financial worries, problems with relations, difficulties caused by work (for example, work which involves being away from home for long periods or which allows little time for husband, wife, and children to be together), "things going wrong" continually. All these put a great deal of strain upon a marriage. Often it is the accumulation of problems and difficulties and their continuance over a long period without relief that cause cracks to appear in a marriage. The counsellor feels that the couple concerned could have successfully borne this anxiety, this problem and even that particular crisis as well, but the husband falling out of work at the same time has been altogether too much and almost any marriage would have been in difficulties. If in such a case the counsellor can relieve one or two of the external pressures, he will ease some of the tension and at least be in a position to see whether beneath it all there is a relationship problem that needs his help. The counsellor must remember what has been said about the indirect approach; he must not conclude because some-one has come to him to talk about real external stresses that the relieving of these will be the end of the matter. On the other hand, he must not be so eager to look further than the obvious as to miss the fact that in this instance the obvious is the real problem. Even if the real problem is to be found elsewhere than in the surface tensions, the lessening of these will help towards the solution.

4

Further Causes of Breakdown

Quarrels

"My husband and I never have a cross word" or "We never quarrel". Whenever this is said to me I suspect one of three things: either he is the boss and she does what he says, and so they never quarrel, or vice versa, or they are leading such emotionally remote and separate lives that they never have any real contact with each other.

This is the kind of reassurance needed by a husband and wife who are brought to the brink of despair by their frequent and sometimes violent quarrelling. We need to emphasize that any couple who are striving to achieve a real partnership are bound to have quarrels. In this sense quarrels are "growing pains". If anyone contests this, let us admit right away that in a perfect state of things quarrels would not occur. But most of us are not in a perfect state of things, and have not progressed very far along the road. From the nature of things there are bound to be quarrels if we are setting out to achieve the highest, a real partnership in a close relationship, with neither partner dominating the other, and each respecting the personality and individuality of the other. If, although unknown to ourselves, we are setting out to achieve something less than a true partnership in a close relationship, then there will be less likelihood of conflict. It could almost be said that the absence of conflict should make a couple look at themselves and examine what their aim in marriage really is.

Having said that to a couple who are in distress over the

rows they have and the form those rows take, there is no need to leave it at that. There is a great deal a counsellor can do. The first thing to do is to try to diagnose why they quarrel. We must bear in mind what has been said about communication, and recognize the frustration that arises in a couple because of an intense desire to communicate when they have not found out how to do so. This is often a cause of violent temper. We can all behave like the child who shakes with fury in his frustration at being unable to communicate. And then we must look for other causes. First, for example, is there a physical cause? The counsellor must be wary of giving the impression that his only concern is to hurry the couple off to a doctor because he is unable or unwilling to cope with them himself. On the other hand it would be stupid of him not to eliminate in his own mind one or two simple things. For example, does the wife suffer from pre-menstrual tension? A few careful questions will show whether she finds life unbearably difficult just before her period and whether it is at this time that the quarrels take place. This is quite often the case. If the counsellor suspects that it is so with the couple who are seeing him, he will suggest that the wife's doctor should be consulted, for pre-menstrual tension is something that a doctor can deal with. But even if the main cause of the quarrelling seems to be this, the counsellor's work will not yet be finished. He will be able, perhaps sometimes better than the doctor, to assist the husband to see and to understand his wife's difficulties and suggest ways in which he can help and support her.

Being in a low state of health is a physical condition that causes quarrels, for when our defences are at a low ebb we probably have enough energy to make a row but not enough to prevent one. Here again, the matter may be one for cooperation between doctor and counsellor.

The apprentice counsellor must not think that the first thing to do is to send his clients off to the doctor. In the great majority of cases he will not need to do so. But he will need to ask one or two questions and to decide whether or not this is one of those occasions when he ought to suggest a medical consultation.

If he decides that in this instance there is no need to suggest a visit to the doctor, the counsellor must then try to find the causes of the quarrels and disagreements. There is no point in his suggesting that the couple should try to control their temper and exercise self-discipline; indeed there is a great deal of point in his not moralizing in this kind of way. For, generally speaking, quarrels and temper are symptoms not causes, and there is about as much point in suggesting to a man and woman that they should control their temper as in a doctor suggesting to a patient with a suppurating appendix that he should control his pain. People are very unbalanced in their attitude to bad temper, especially in others. For example, Mrs A. is a woman who "blows her top", screams at her husband and children, and is always making scenes. Everyone says how "bad" she is and how terrible she must be to live with. Her neighbour, Mrs B., never loses her temper with anyone, but at least once a week spends a day in bed with a migraine. Everyone feels so sorry for her. Yet both the temper and the migraine are stress symptoms. If the woman with the temper is to be blamed, then we must also blame the woman with the migraine. If the latter deserves all our sympathy, then so does the former. Why are we so censorious over one person's outlet, temper, and so accepting of other people's outlets, the pub, the club, the obsession, the withdrawal, the migraine, headache, backache, and so on?

It is obvious that people's tempers are shorter when they are tired, and in the early years of marriage a couple can become very tired. If the wife goes on with her job until the first baby arrives, then instead of coming home to a meal all ready for them and a minimum of household chores and responsibilities, as they used to do when they were single, they now come home to an empty house, have to get the meal themselves, and then have to set about the work needed to keep a house going. They soon discover how much there is to do in a house, and until they have learnt to adjust themselves to the situation it can be very exacting for a young couple to have to do this at the end of a day's work. If the husband has grown up accustomed to think that the work about the house is the woman's work, then additional pressure is put on the wife, who besides feeling more tired than she has ever done before, probably chafes under the unfairness of things and uses up any shreds of energy she may have left in dealing with the ensuing mental conflict. The counsellor can help the couple to see their situation and encourage the husband to realize that while they are both out at work and earning for the home, they both equally have the responsibilities for the household chores. He can also help them to see that it is tiredness and not waning affection that is causing them to quarrel.

By accepting this they will at least be spared the additional strain of despair and anxiety about how things are going. All this may seem very simple and very obvious, but the experienced counsellor will know that it is not always obvious and never simple to those involved in the situation.

To most couples the arrival of the first baby will bring joy; to all couples it will certainly bring unlooked-for strain and unimagined tiredness. The extra work that a baby makes and the loss of sleep, sometimes night after night, can be very wearing, and it is not surprising if husband and wife become edgy and their tempers shorter.

Anxiety can cause tempers to fray, especially when the connection between the anxiety and the shortness of the temper is not recognized. If a man can say to himself, "I have been worried about this situation at work and that is why my wife says I'm unbearable to live with and am always snapping her head off", then he can be on the way to becoming less unbearable to live with. If he is full of anxiety but pushes it down in his mind and refuses to see the effect it is having upon him, then his wife and children, and other people generally are likely to become the objects of his bad temper.

For here the phenomenon called "projection" comes into operation. Unable to face or deal with the real anxiety or fear, he will project it on to someone or something else and deal with it there. He is unconsciously saying to himself, "The trouble isn't this, it is that. I cannot bear the thought of what it is, I must transpose it into something else that I can deal with more easily." And so, not being in a position to storm at his boss, he will shout at his wife instead. In common parlance we say that "He takes it out on her" or "She has to suffer for it". Wives also are not exempt from the phenomenon of projection. If she has had a trying day with the children or her mother-in-law and feels she has not handled the situation adequately, then her husband is likely, as we say, to "catch it" when he comes in.

"Danger—Projection at Work" is a hazard sign that could well be written over every front door. It is not, perhaps, so dangerous when the trouble is overt and can be easily recognized. It is comparatively easy for a wife to say, "Something has gone wrong in the office, I expect", or for the husband to see that she is "letting fly" at him because she has been worried about the baby and her nerves are all on edge. Projection is much more difficult to recognize, and therefore much more dangerous, when the anxiety is what we often loosely call a "psychological" one; when some deep well-spring of emotion has been touched and deep-down fears, apprehensions, and even terrors are stirred within us. Usually they are unknown to us and unrecognized by us, and then the unity, peace, and concord of the home are threatened. For we can relieve the tension within us by projecting it on to a wife or husband (or someone else) outside us. And we do not know what is happening. For we can usually find a peg to hang our projection on—something in the other person that we consider to be wrong and that we can use to build up into the thing that is upsetting us. Unable to deal with the disturbance inside us we project it on to our partner and chastise it there.

The counsellor needs to be aware of the phenomenon of

projection and be asking himself whether or not this is what is happening in the marriage which is his present concern. He can explain to the two partners how the human mind, unable to bear more than a certain degree of anxiety, can project it elsewhere and he can give illustrations of this. From here he can proceed to suggest that this may well be what has been happening on some occasions in their own marriage; and if they can begin to recognize projection at work when it is easy to see it, perhaps they can learn to become aware that this may be happening on other occasions also, and gradually recognize those occasions when they arise.

It helps the recipient of the projected anxiety (the wife, let us say, who is the temporary object of her husband's fury), if she can say to herself, "He is upset or worried or disturbed and he is getting rid of it on to me. I'll try to help him get over it." Later she may be able to discover why her husband is so upset, and, perhaps, by sharing the worry with him help him to bear it. The husband in his turn, aware of the phenomenon of projection, later on when he has come to himself, may be able to see that he was off-loading all his anxiety on to his wife, and by admitting this to her be able to unsay some of the bitter and hurtful words he has flung at her.

A couple may be comforted by the thought that it is often easier to off-load things on to people we love and who love us than on to people with whom we are not in a close relationship. Those who do not love us would not stand it for thirty seconds; it is sometimes a measure of the confidence that we have in our mutual love and in the stability of our relationship that we can throw so much of our anxiety on to each other.

It is obvious that jealousy is the cause of much bitter quarrelling. That it is the means by which one partner exercises a tyranny over the other is also obvious to everyone except the jealous partner. Just as obvious, too, is the fact that it is quite useless to say to a man, "You mustn't be so jealous." He cannot help feeling jealous. Should he attempt to suppress his jealous feelings and acquiesce in behaviour on the part of his wife which would usually, though to the outsider quite irrationally, arouse such feelings of jealousy in him, this would result only in the temporary damming up of torrents of emotions, later to burst out in even greater floods. It is more to the point for the counsellor to help the husband to see the kind of tyranny he is exercising and help the wife to see how very painful and largely beyond his control her husband's feelings are. The counsellor can then encourage the wife, on the one hand, to concede a good deal, but not all, to her husband's feelings, and the husband, on the other, to deny some but not all of his jealousy. The wife will take her husband's feelings into account and act with gentleness and understanding; but she will not let herself be enslaved by her husband's unreasonable jealousy, for to do so might be a short-term gain but would certainly be a long-term disaster. The husband will learn that there is a certain amount of jealous feeling that he can be expected to endure without complaint; the wife, for her part, will accept the fact that she must not press her husband beyond the point of endurance. If the wife does her part and the husband his, then the confidence born of such an understanding will probably in course of time cause the problem to diminish.

However relevant such counselling may be, it is even more relevant if we can make it a means of discovering the cause in the person himself of the jealous feelings that arise unbidden and unwanted. Very often jealous feelings arise from a deep-buried sense of deprivation, emptiness, and littleness, built into the personality by experience and environment. If the wife can counteract this feeling of emptiness by giving her husband a sense of fullness in their relationship, and the husband through knowledge of himself can see where his problem lies and can seek his own solution to it, the jealousy is being tackled at source. In this case both cause and symptom are being dealt with.

The subject of sex will need a separate section, but here it is worth noticing the connection between quarrelling and sexual frustration. If a woman, for example, is stimulated by sexual intercourse but is left at the end of it unsatisfied, her orgasm unachieved, the next day she may well be edgy and quarrelsome and precipitate a first-class row. All the emotion roused in her by sexual encounter must have some outlet, and if for some reason the natural release in orgasm is denied her, then she will give vent to her feelings in other ways. For her the ensuing row will be a kind of orgasm. A man also can be sexually frustrated, perhaps by a wife's failure to respond to his love-making; his frustration may well express itself in violent quarrelling.

When people quarrel, self-justification accompanied by re-crimination is natural. Who is wrong, and who ought to put things right, are the considerations that are uppermost in a person's mind. The counsellor can suggest to a couple that when things go wrong it is more helpful to concentrate not on who put them wrong but how they can be put right. If both partners are engaged in self-justification and are standing on their rights, it is usually easier for the one who technically is more "in the right" to abandon his position and accept the blame and the responsibility, or at least some of it. The partner who is "in the wrong" but does not admit it is usually inhibited by unacknowledged feelings of guilt, and has not so much freedom of movement as the one who is less in the wrong. The one who is in the secure position of being able to say to himself "I did not cause this quarrel" is much freer to set about restoring the situation by accepting the blame and thus relieving the other of the guilt. This assumption of guilt should, of course, be a temporary measure to bridge the gap caused by the quarrel; it should be recognized by the other partner as the loving generosity that it is, and lead to an admission of responsibility in turn.

Occasions of Breakdown

Marriages can, of course, break down at any time. There are, however, certain stages which are more dangerous to marriage than others. There are times that most couples find particularly difficult and it is in one of these that an already insecure marriage is especially at risk. Even if such a marriage manages to survive the first one or two difficult periods, nevertheless patterns may be formed that will lead to breakdown later.

The first year or so of a marriage is one obviously dangerous period. The difficulties of adjustment; the coming to understand what marriage is not, as well as what it is; sexual problems, perhaps quite small in themselves; these all make this a time of unsettlement and uncertainty and therefore a time of danger. In some marriages, the realization of the responsibility that has been undertaken and the commitment entered into is more important than anything else. The weight of responsibility is a great strain for some young couples and their marriage creaks and cracks, if it does not break up, under it. It is in the first months of a marriage that external pressures, such as relationships with in-laws and friends, can be very great.

It is not often that a marriage actually breaks down during its first year, but it not infrequently happens that at this time the seeds of breakdown are sown. If only it were an accepted fact that a normal couple would want to go to an experienced marriage counsellor at some time during their first year to discuss their initial difficulties or even just to talk about marriage now that they have had some experience of it, how much distress and misery would be prevented. How often after a consultation does a counsellor say to himself: "If only they had gone to someone five or ten or even forty years ago, how easy it would have been to have dealt with the problem then and how many years of unhappiness they would have been spared; but now it is almost, if not quite, insoluble." Society is gradually, though only very gradually, becoming aware of the importance of marriage preparation, pre-marriage discussion groups, and pre-marriage counselling; unfortunately it seems to regard a visit by a young married couple to a marriage counsellor as "Not right", something "we wouldn't want anyone to know about". Such a visit is regarded as an admission of failure, perhaps as a last desperate measure, the final recognition and admission that the marriage has failed. I can recall one young couple having the sense to come along early in their marriage to talk about something that was then a simple matter of adjustment, and what a difference a brief consultation made to their marriage. They were followed a few hours afterwards by a woman who had been married thirty years. She poured out such a history of unhappiness and misery and gave such a picture of her marriage that all it seemed possible to hope for was the salvaging of a few scraps from the wreckage. I asked her a few questions to try to discover where and how things had gone wrong and I remember vividly realizing that in her case the trouble had started in the early months of her marriage and with the same simple problem of adjustment which had been brought to me by the young couple who had left a few hours before. I needed no further assurance of the need for seeking help from a marriage counsellor in the early days of difficulty. Most people do seek advice, of course, haphazardly from the man on the shop floor or from the woman in the office, but this is not the same thing. It seems that almost every married couple could benefit from talking things over from time to time with an experienced counsellor.

The arrival of the first baby is another crisis period in a marriage. The couple are now tied and have to adapt themselves to an entirely different way of life. They cannot go out together without finding a baby-sitter, and that is no easy matter if they are not living near relatives, and it is sometimes difficult even if they are. The effort needed in order to go out together hardly seems worth it. So Monday becomes her night out and Tuesday and Friday his. The baby makes continual demands upon them for which they are little prepared; broken nights and the ensuing tiredness strain their nerves and leave them no energy for the enjoyment of each other's company. The change for the wife is particularly great. The husband still goes on with his job, but the wife has to give up her work and the friends she has made at work and is now housebound. Day after day she is on her own with only the baby as a companion and the local shopkeeper and a neighbour with whom to exchange an occasional word. If our society wishes to punish someone severely, it condemns him to solitary confinement, which is precisely what we condemn many of our young wives to for most of the day. Then we wonder why they are on edge and difficult to live with! The arrival of the first baby, then, is going to demand a great deal of readjustment on the part of husband and wife. For the wife things cannot go on as before and if her husband does not understand how different and difficult her life is and does not adapt himself to give her all the support he can, then it will be at this time that they will begin to grow apart, though they may not be aware of what is happening to them.

A not infrequent phenomenon after the birth of the first baby is the husband's jealousy of his own child, his resentment of the attention and mothering that his wife is giving to their baby. The reasons are deep down and psychological and the husband may not be able to put his feelings into words. The counsellor, however, must be aware that a husband can react in this way. What we have said about jealousy above applies here too, though for obvious reasons the matter is more urgent. A discussion with the husband of his view of marriage and how he sees his relationship with his wife can be useful, for it sometimes gives the counsellor an opportunity not only of dealing with the problem of jealousy but also of helping the husband to see that he is basically looking for a second mother in his partner. Although she may fulfil this role for some of the time, the man who is looking only for this in his wife is to that extent immature. Even the recognition of the need to mature can, I find, be therapeutic.

The counsellor must also know that after childbirth the woman can suffer from what doctors call "puerperal depression". This is a medical condition, and the right person to help her is the doctor. The patient may be what we call in common speech "depressed", or she may show signs of anxiety or agitation. If the wife is "not herself", the situation at home will be difficult for both her and her husband. If they should come to a counsellor and he has the faintest suspicion that this may be a puerperal depression, he should without hesitation suggest a medical consultation. He will still, however, be able to give to the couple a good deal of support and by his relationship with them as well as by his counselling help them through their bad patch.

It is evident that at this time sexual problems may arise. Sometimes the woman's desire for intercourse wanes and her enjoyment of it diminishes. This may be due to a latent fear of another pregnancy (though this is not always so), weariness, and the disturbance that a baby causes. A good deal of readjustment is likely to be needed on this side of a couple's marriage, and this is likely to cause some difficulty.

The trials of the menopause are well known, yet it is surprising how often wives, husbands, and doctors are unaware of its onset. For sometimes an emotional disturbance occurs before there is sufficient physical evidence to impinge on the mind, and the thing about emotional disturbance is that it disturbs, in this instance, the wife and her husband. Once the couple understand the situation they can accept it and adapt themselves to it, though often not easily. The trouble arises when, as so frequently happens, the couple have been living in an upsetting situation for some time before its cause has been recognized, and this happens even when the woman has been going to her doctor regularly with complaints of "nerves", or aches and pains, or of being generally run-down. When a counsellor is approached by a middle-aged husband or wife he should always bear in mind that the main trouble may be the menopause and tentatively ask if this could be so. He should proceed gently, as always, because while one part of the woman will accept the situation with relief, as the explanation of why she has found life so difficult lately, the other part of her may resist the thought that she has reached the "change of life". For this to her is synonymous with "getting old". It is a "change of life" to which she does not look forward. A question to the husband, on the other hand, about the possibility of the menopause being the reason for his wife's being so difficult to live with may evoke the response, "Don't tell me it's her age; she's always been like that." There may be some truth in this, though it is probably not the whole truth. For a woman's difficulties or personality problems will be accentuated during the time of the menopause. If she has always been inclined to be "highly strung" and "on edge", she will be even more so now. But this means just as much that the need she has always felt, to be loved by and to be important to her husband, will be greater now. A husband's need is to be helped to see this.

At this time there is almost certainly some sexual adjustment to be made. The woman may lose her desire for intercourse and her enjoyment of it. Sometimes this may be because her main interest in intercourse has, perhaps unconsciously, been her desire to have children. She can be helped to see this and to adjust to the new situation. In any case, whatever the reason for her diminished interest in sex, because of it her fear that she is growing old will be reinforced and she may well think that life is over for her. If her husband by patience, affection, and understanding sees her through this period, not only will their relationship take on a quality they never imagined possible, but their lovemaking is likely to became something they both enjoy more and find more meaningful than before.

The counsellor must also take into account the seldom-recognized fact that in middle age the man also goes through a very difficult period, his own kind of "change of life". He too feels that he is "growing old" and cannot do all the things he used to do. His children begin to outstrip him physically and possibly intellectually and he cannot cut the figure in his family that he once did.[1] He realizes that he has got as far in

[1] This raises, I know, the whole question of the man's position in the family. As the children grow up, the family should develop from being a

his career as he is going to get, and that he may not be nearly as far as he had hoped or imagined; he now has to watch younger men go ahead of him. Consequently, many middle-aged men are "disappointed men" (words in common use about men of this age). What has sustained them in life has been their desire to "get on" and to achieve status and security. Their drive to "get on" and to achieve status now loses its meaning and a waning physical capacity threatens their security. Small wonder then that middle-aged men often go through a period of quite serious depression and frustration and are such a trial to live with.

A middle-aged man's awareness of his diminishing physical powers may produce in him a pathetic attempt at a juvenile comeback. He will be attracted to young women because he wants to feel that he can still attract them. His sexual powers do not wane, indeed they may increase at the same time as his wife's interest in sex is, temporarily, decreasing.

Enough has been said to show why the marriage of a middle-aged couple is at a difficult, if not a critical, stage. The difficulty is aggravated if it is at this time that their children are leaving home either to get married themselves or in pursuit of their various careers. For the time when their children leave home constitutes another difficult period for a married couple. If it coincides with the onset of the problems of middle age, it will exacerbate those problems; if it comes later, it will still mean that another stage of re-assessment and re-adjustment has to be negotiated. The impoverishment of a husband and wife's relationship is often masked by their absorption in their family. The children have been coming and going and in one way or another occupying a good deal of attention. Now husband and wife are on their own and they can no longer escape from seeing how little there is left between them. Evening after evening they sit opposite each

---

paternal into being a fraternal community. If it has done so, the man will not be faced with this problem at this stage. More often than not, however, this development has not taken place.

other unable to avoid facing their life's biggest failure. Eventually he escapes into unending rounds of golf and similar activities from which his wife is excluded, while she goes to bingo or to a variety of pastimes in which her husband takes no part.

At least now they know the truth about their relationship. Should one or both of them be driven, either by unhappiness or the desire to do something about the situation, to seek help from a counsellor, the latter can have the confidence of knowing that at this stage in their marriage and starting from this point of realizing that they have not much left between them, many couples have built up a very warm and worthwhile relationship.

5
Sex

Recently I asked a Young Wives' Group, about thirty in number, to divide into small groups to discuss and answer various questions. One question was: In how many marriages is there a sex problem of one kind or another at one time or another? The answers were consistent that in from 80% to 100% of marriages there is a sex problem at some time.

A young couple with a sexual difficulty needs a lot of re-assurance, and it is very reassuring to them to be told that it is "normal" for a couple to have a sex problem. The counsellor can almost hear them saying with relief, "Thank God we're normal . . . normal . . . normal!" Of course theirs may be one of the severe sexual problems that we shall be considering in a moment; but, even if it is, a little reassurance at this stage will not come amiss. Many couples take a long time, often as much as two or three years, to achieve sexual harmony. A couple need to be told this and encouraged to work at making their marriage a happy one in this respect as well as in others. Fear of failure is likely to be present and adds considerably to the distress of the situation. If, however, they refuse to give up and just make do with things as they are, then they can be encouraged to believe that all will be well and well worth waiting for.

When dealing with a sexual problem we must ask (as with so many other problems in counselling) whether this is cause or effect. Is the sexual difficulty causing discord in the relationship, or is an unsatisfactory relationship producing the sexual disharmony? It could be one or the other, or a com-

bination of both. For in sex the whole of the personality is
engaged. An unsatisfactory sexual encounter disorganizes the
relationship of the couple, and then the disturbed relationship in its turn makes the sexual engagement more difficult
and less satisfying.

If the relationship of the couple concerned seems to us
basically a good one and the sexual problem a comparatively
minor one, then we may be confident that the sex difficulty
is a cause and not a symptom and needs our main attention.
If, on the other hand, the sexual problem is a severe one,
then we may diagnose either that it began as a minor difficulty but has gone on so long unresolved that it has now become both severe and chronic and has gravely affected the
relationship, or that we are dealing with a serious relationship or personality problem and probably a mixture of both.

Frigidity

Frigidity in a woman can be mild or severe. It is mild if it is
simply a matter of adjustment, like learning how to make
love successfully, minor physical difficulties that a doctor can
put right, discomfort, and simple and uncomplicated forms
of those stresses that cause frigidity in its severe form; it is
severe if it involves some deep emotional personality or
relationship problem.

Mild frigidity can from custom become chronic and even
severe if it is not dealt with in its early stages. And frequently
it is not tackled at all either early or late. This is because
even in these so-called enlightened days the attitude of many
women is that sex is something which is all right for a man
but which a woman has to put up with. This is still a very
common attitude among women and is perpetuated by being
passed on as the experience of one generation to the next.
Consequently if a young wife does not immediately enjoy
intercourse or even finds it distasteful, she often does noth-

ing about it because she has been conditioned not to expect any enjoyment from it.[1]

A husband can be a very poor lover out of sheer ignorance of how his wife likes him to approach her and make love to her. This is very often the cause of a wife's coldness. We have already considered this in the section on "Communication" and there is no need to repeat what has been said there. It is impossible to lay down hard and fast rules on "how to make love", for a man is not making love to women in general but to this woman in particular. This is all the more reason why a woman should help her husband to understand her and how to make love to her.

Speaking generally, however, a woman does not like being rushed into intercourse, but likes to be wooed and courted and made love to slowly, affectionately, and lovingly. "He only wants me when we go to bed and then he wonders why I'm not interested" is a complaint we often hear. A husband needs to be told (for he is unlikely to realize this on his own) that if he wants to make love to his wife at night, the best time to start is in the morning, by being affectionate and attentive then. The attention and affection should continue when he comes in from work. If he has ignored his wife all day, it is too late to notice her existence for the first time when they go to bed. He is unlikely to awaken much response in her, except of a kind he does not much relish. For, again speaking generally, a woman not only wants to *be* loved but to *feel* loved. For her to find intercourse wholly satisfying it must be a part of that loving that she has already experienced. She has little interest in sex as a thing apart.

Very occasionally we come across the woman whose complaint is that her husband does not make love to her quickly enough and who actually dislikes the slow build-up of love play; but she is an exception.

---

[1] Readers may question whether this really is the outlook of many modern young women. To my great surprise I meet it much more than I would have imagined possible in this day and age.

One cause of mild frigidity is sheer ignorance about the physical side of sex. This is not true frigidity and is comparatively easily remedied, especially with the help of a counsellor.

Another cause of mild frigidity is what may be termed the situation and circumstances of love-making. I remember one woman saying to me, "The bed creaks." She was living with her in-laws and had no sense of privacy and relaxation when her husband made love to her. Some couples do not seem to mind this, but others do. Most people find it necessary to feel that there is not the slightest intrusion upon their privacy.

This is one example of a situation affecting love-making. The counsellor should discover whether circumstances of a similar or a different kind are telling against a couple.

To some it may seem almost unbelievable, but the counsellor sometimes has to come to the conclusion that one of the reasons why intercourse is not proving satisfactory for a couple is that they are not practising it enough. The art of making love has to be learnt and practised like any other art, if it is to be something more than mediocre and is to grow to perfection. If they do not find it perfect straight away some couples will shy away from the encounter and from the sense of failure and frustration that it brings them. They are not prepared to make the effort involved (learning to make love does involve effort), and so intercourse for them becomes haphazard and less frequent. They allow less and less time for it, staying up later and later and going to bed too tired for each other and too tired to give their love-making a chance of being successful.

Often the fear of pregnancy prevents a woman from enjoying intercourse. If the fear of becoming pregnant is lurking somewhere at the back of her mind, she will hardly be able to relax enough to delight in her husband's love-making. She may be fitted with an adequate contraceptive, but if she is all the time wondering whether it is really safe, she is not going to be able to give herself wholly and unrestrainedly to love-making. This problem usually concerns a woman who has had a baby and does not want to begin another immediately, or a mother who does not want any more children. Sometimes, however, a newly-married wife has a deep fear of pregnancy and this tells heavily against her enjoyment of intercourse. If the counsellor finds this to be the case, he is clearly dealing with an entirely different problem. He must try to discover why she has this fear and how far it is an abnormal fear of pregnancy (for most women have some fear), and then he must act accordingly.

Intercourse before marriage can sometimes be the cause of mild frigidity after marriage. If intercourse has taken place before marriage its enjoyment may well be prejudiced by many of the things we have considered above. The circumstances and situation in all likelihood will have been far from ideal, and true, carefree relaxation impossible. In the girl's mind there will probably have been some fear both of pregnancy and discovery; and she may well have had guilt-feelings, although these may have been stifled and unacknowledged. If intercourse has been taking place like this for some time, by the day of the wedding it will by habit have acquired associations which make for anything but the real enjoyment of it. Marriage cannot overnight cause it to lose the associations which it has had for so long. Indeed, if the couple do not face the situation and deal with it, intercourse may be associated throughout their life with anxiety, distaste, and guilt.

If the act of pre-marital intercourse has only been occasional, and if, as is likely, it has not been entirely satisfactory, the couple's love-making will have suffered because they have not been able to practise it more often. (We have already seen the effect of infrequent love-making even in the case of married couples.) By the time of the wedding the girl will "know from experience" what intercourse is going to be like and enter into marriage prepared to accept that unsatisfactory situation.

If intercourse before marriage has been pleasurable and successful for both the man and the woman, this is no guarantee that it will continue to be so when they are married. Again circumstances enter in. If, for example, fear of discovery, instead of being a bar to enjoyment, has been one of the ingredients of the enjoyment (the "Forbidden Fruit" syndrome), if pleasurable love-making has been associated with the circumstances in which it took place before marriage, then the circumstances after marriage, when the couple are "fully licensed", as it were, are going to be quite different. Some couples find it difficult to adjust to the changed circumstances.

The counsellor will find, when a couple come to him for help, that they will rarely hesitate to speak about their experience before marriage, providing that a relationship of trust has been established with him, that they respect his skill as a counsellor, and have confidence that whatever questions he asks are not to satisfy his own curiosity or to enable him to pry unnecessarily into their lives but to help him to help them. Above all he must not moralize.

Perhaps a word of caution is necessary here. We may jump to the conclusion that intercourse before marriage always has disastrous effects after marriage. This is certainly not so. The counsellor, however, must bear in mind the fact that pre-marital intercourse can for one or other of the reasons outlined above be a cause of dissatisfaction with intercourse in marriage.

So far we have considered what I have termed "mild" frigidity, that is frigidity which is not deep-seated, and which is capable of comparatively easy remedy. (I stress the word "comparatively". No remedy is easy, except by comparison.) Severe frigidity is an entirely different matter. The symptoms may be the same, but their origins are different.

Severe frigidity almost always has its roots deep in the emotions, usually in the unconscious emotions, in experiences we have forgotten because we cannot bear to remember them. We can all of us remember things that have happened to us, perhaps long ago in childhood when we were at our most impressionable, experiences pleasant or frightening which are affecting our present attitudes and actions. I know a man of fifty who always puts on his right shoe first and would feel very ill at ease if by some inadvertency (impossible for him to imagine) he should do the opposite. He can remember exactly when and why he began to do so. He can recall as a child of six hearing a schoolteacher tell a story about Richard the First and saying: "Richard was a very brave king; when he went out to battle if he had put on his right boot first he would say, 'This is good luck, we are going to win'; but if he had put on his left boot first he would say, 'This is bad luck, we are going to lose.' " My friend can remember wondering, even at the age of six, how this made Richard a brave king and why he never made certain of always putting on his right boot first. However, the incident made such an impression on him that today without thinking he invariably puts on his right shoe first and would find it impossible to do otherwise. We can all think of things that have affected us like this. But what of those experiences which have made an indelible impression upon us and which have affected us deeply, but which we cannot now remember? Suppose my friend had forgotten the incident of the schoolteacher's story, he would today be taking measures to avoid ever putting on his left shoe first and neither he nor anyone else would be able to understand why.

With severe frigidity we must assume that its origin is to be found in a hurtful experience in the past. Perhaps a child depending upon and trusting in someone completely and then hurt beyond bearing (by someone who may be completely unaware of the damage he does) is conditioned by the experience never to commit herself wholly to anyone again. This is now her way of life, always to be on the defensive and to keep something of herself back. In order to enjoy intercourse and to find it wholly satisfying she will have to commit herself unreservedly to her husband and lose herself in his loving. But this is precisely what she cannot do. She has been able to trust her husband sufficiently to love him and to marry him, but has been unable to give herself to him completely.

Or perhaps a child from a very tender age has had it impressed upon her that sex before marriage is a terrible thing, until her reaction is that it is better not to have too much to do with something so frightening. Her love for her husband and her desire for marriage have been strong enough to induce her to endure in silence the distaste she feels for sex, for the sake of getting married. Such endurance is unlikely to last long.

It is not uncommon to find that premarital chastity has been taught in such a way that a girl has become inhibited with regard to sex.

The subject of frigidity needs, not a chapter on its own, but a book on its own. We certainly cannot deal fully with the subject here. If the counsellor has acquired a great deal of knowledge, technique, and experience he may feel able to deal with a case of severe frigidity himself. I once interviewed a woman who quite clearly found it impossible to commit herself wholly and completely. After a number of interviews we seemed to have made no progress until one day she returned and said, "After I'd left you I remembered something that I'd quite forgotten. I remember when I was very young, too young, I suppose, for my mother to think I could understand, I overheard my mother say to a friend, 'I ran all the way down to the village shop to try to get rid of her but I couldn't, so I had to have her.'" To which I said, "You were an unwanted baby, weren't you? Your own mother didn't want you." At this she broke down completely, but knowing at last the truth about herself and her relationship with her mother, she began to be free from the bondage in which in ignorance she had been held. Since then she has found life, if not easy, yet a good deal easier. If a counsellor has sufficient experience to help someone in this way, he will have sufficient experience to know when he needs to pass his client on to someone with specialist knowledge, either specialist medical knowledge or specialist counselling knowledge.

So far I have only briefly mentioned the possibility of there being a physical cause for frigidity. Clearly this is a possibility which a counsellor must bear in mind. The inexperienced counsellor is apt either to hurry his client off to the doctor when there is no evidence that such a visit is desirable and plenty of evidence that factors other than the physical ones are involved; or he will endeavour to deal on his own with a matter that is outside his province. It is difficult to decide which in the end causes more distress to the client.

Impotence

Medical opinion is not entirely certain about the factors that cause impotence in younger men. Some doctors say that it is unlikely to have a physical cause and therefore not much can be done to alleviate the condition by physical means. Others may be more inclined to look for an organic element. There seems, however, to be agreement that there is likely to be a large psychological element present, and some would say that the cause of impotence is more likely to be psychological than constitutional.

Impotence in older men is different. Here the physical conditions of increasing age, illness, tiredness are more likely to be the causes, though the counsellor should be open to the possibility that there may be a problem of relationship between husband and wife.

Impotence in her husband is often a source of great distress to a wife as well as to the husband concerned. In addition to anguish for other reasons, the wife may suspect that her husband does not find her attractive enough and that this is the reason why he is unable to make love to her. This is seldom the case, and the counsellor can help by being reassuring on this point. He can help the wife to understand her husband's difficulty and help the husband to understand himself. As we saw when discussing frigidity in women, if the counsellor is sufficiently experienced and has an adequate knowledge of the problem with which he is dealing, he may not find it necessary to call in specialist help. Most counsellors, however, will feel the need to do so. In any event the counsellor will be able to help the couple considerably by his friendship, understanding, and support.

Deviations

The word sometimes used here is "perversions". This word, however, has emotional overtones which, implying judgement, are out of place in a counsellor's thinking. The number of deviations a counsellor may come across is legion, and in its context that is probably the right way to describe them.

Male homosexuality is one such deviation. Constitutionally few men are entirely homosexual and few are entirely heterosexual. Some are largely heterosexual with a small homosexual element in them, some the reverse. The degrees of homosexuality and heterosexuality vary from man to man. A man who has a large homosexual element in him may be quite capable of entering into marriage, but having committed himself to a relationship with a woman may have great difficulty in making a success of that relationship.

Homosexuality in women is less common as a cause of marriage breakdown, but is occasionally found to be the cause of trouble in a marriage.

As in the case of impotence, doctors do not agree about the cause of either male or female homosexuality. Indeed medical opinion is sharply divided between those who look for an organic and those who look for psychological cause. Most doctors would look for a physical cause in the case of a middle-aged man becoming fond of young boys or showing other symptoms of homosexuality and would attribute this to glandular changes or some other physical condition, for example, arterio-sclerosis. A possible view is that homosexuality has both a constitutional and a psychological element. A man may have a constitutional predisposition to homosexuality; given a good psychological upbringing and environment his homosexuality may remain latent and he may be able to enter into marriage entirely successfully. An upbringing and environment creating stress and distress may give greater significance to that homosexuality to which he is constitutionally predisposed. Even if it does not lead to homosexual acts, it may be a large enough factor to make a relationship in marriage difficult. If he has been able to contract a marriage, later stress, particularly in the marriage relationship itself, may cause an already stressed individual to have what may be termed a homosexual breakdown.

Sadism and masochism are more commonly found as problems in marriage. In their mild forms the counsellor will meet them quite often. In their more severe expressions he will come across them less frequently, though enough to prevent him from ever being able to ignore their existence. Here the person concerned is so conditioned that he is unable to achieve sexual satisfaction with anyone, except by the infliction or reception of pain. The attitude is "better a painful relationship than no relationship at all". As sexuality is both the expression of relationship and the attempt to achieve relationship, it must for this person have its concomitant of pain.

The counsellor will certainly meet other deviations, for example, the desire for *fellatio* (oral intercourse). The lines of approach indicated in this chapter will be those to follow: What are the underlying causes of these symptoms? Can I help this couple both with support and treatment; or, while giving them support, do I need to call in specialist advice?

Masturbation

It is necessary to say something about masturbation because it sometimes causes disquiet in a marriage. I hope, however, that the mentioning of it does not give it a prominence or importance it does not deserve.

A wife will sometimes be upset because she knows or suspects that her husband is masturbating. More than once I have heard a complaint made about this in a court of law and the wife claiming that this shows her husband is "perverted". If a wife does not react in this way, she may nevertheless wonder what is wrong with herself that her husband sometimes masturbates instead of seeking intercourse with her. A husband, on the other hand, may be disturbed by his own masturbation and have guilt feelings about it.

Masturbation is a symptom and not a disease. It is one of the ways in which people comfort themselves. (There are many ways of comforting oneself, for example with smoking, alcohol, snacks, tranquillizers, or cups of tea.) They learn this way of self-comfort when young and may never entirely lose it. As their inner tension abates so does the masturbation. If a man, with the help of a counsellor, can resolve his interior stress, his habit of masturbation will diminish and fade away. As inner stress is often resolved in a satisfying relationship, if a counsellor can help a couple towards a better relationship, one of the "fringe benefits" of his counselling will be the solving of a masturbation problem.

Infidelity

As in other instances in this book, we have to ask whether infidelity is a cause of marriage breakdown or whether it is a sign that a marriage is already breaking down or has broken down.

Sometimes the counsellor will find that marriage has been entered into by one or both partners with the conviction that an occasional, temporary sexual liaison outside marriage does not matter and has nothing to do with the marriage relationship. Certainly I have met this attitude myself, combined with a round condemnation of those who are promiscuous. Whatever we may think of it, we must recognize that such an attitude does not cause distress if it is genuinely accepted by both partners. It does cause distress when it is the viewpoint of one only.

We frequently meet with the situation in which one partner, to the great distress of the other, has committed adultery.
This may have been on a single occasion, or on several occasions; the partner may be sorry it has happened or quite un-
repentant; he may be in confusion as to what his real feelings
are; he may have formed what he intends to be a permanent
relationship with someone else. Naturally our counselling
will vary according to the circumstances.

The counsellor will want to discover what has brought
about the infidelity. What has the husband, for example,
found in someone else that he could not or did not find in
his wife? What has the wife felt lacking in her marriage that
she sought elsewhere? Did the husband look in vain to his
wife for affection and understanding? Did the wife feel that
she was treated like a "piece of furniture" (wives often use
these words), so that she fell for the first man who noticed
her, made a fuss of her, and treated her as a person? Had
either of them drifted into a relationship unawares? "I didn't
realize what was happening" is a common description of how
a casual meeting developed gradually into an impossible
situation.

In helping to mend a marriage which has been battered
by the discovery of sexual infidelity, a counsellor knows that
the first thing both partners need is a great deal of reassurance before mutual forgiveness can be properly offered
or accepted.

The wife, for example, will want to be reassured that her
husband really means it when he says that he still loves her.
She can be helped to see, for instance, that it is all too easy
for a man, confident of his own steadfastness, to drift im-
perceptibly into a relationship with another woman, unaware that such a thing could happen to him; having learnt
from bitter experience how such a situation can develop, he
is unlikely ever again to act in the same way, now being able
to recognize the earliest signs and to be on his guard. The
wife can be greatly reassured and begin to have confidence
in her husband again if she can see and understand this.

The "guilty" partner can be helped to accept himself, and both partners can be encouraged to see that "infidelity", as it is commonly called, is by no means the worst of all infidelities, and not the most destructive of a marriage; other things not normally listed as "infidelity" can be in fact much more "unfaithful" and do much more harm to a marriage relationship.

Sometimes a husband may ask what there is special and unique about the relationship between himself and his wife now that "she has given to another man everything she has given to me". The answer is that she has not given to another all that she has given to her husband. She has not, for example, committed herself in marriage to another man. There may have been sex, but it has been sex without commitment, and it is the commitment more than the sex which makes the relationship between a husband and wife special and unique. The relationship that a man has with his wife is different from any other relationship; it may be a better or a worse relationship, but it is not the same; it is "special" to them both.

This kind of reassurance can be comforting to a couple trying to build up their marriage again out of apparent ruins.

"But I'm not in love with her any more. I wish I were", a husband will sometimes say; or, "She says she doesn't love me." The answer in the former case is that he fell in love with her once and there is no reason why he should not do so again, and in the latter that he made her fall in love with him before, now he must woo her anew.

A husband and wife often need to be told that they can fall in love again if they give themselves time to do so, and if they are prepared to court each other all over again. They must not expect to feel in love with each other immediately; they may do so but they must not expect it; they must be prepared to wait. They can look back and see how they fell in love the first time. He can remember how he grew to know her and how he courted her (the counsellor can help him to remember how much attention he paid her then and how much time he

gave up to winning her), and she can recall how she set out
to make herself attractive to him. Now they must start again.

A couple can be encouraged to feel that it is quite an adven-
ture courting each other again, going out together to a meal
or an entertainment, and making time for this, something
that they may not have done for years. Patience is essential.
It is difficult for them because they want to feel at once that
everything is right between them. They must realize that it
will take time.

A relationship which has been shattered by deeds can seldom be put right by words. Words will be needed, but without deeds they will not be believed. Usually it takes a deed
to undo a deed. A trust that has been destroyed can only be
restored gradually. If a husband complains that his wife will
not trust him, then he must be encouraged to be patient until
he has given her grounds for trusting him. He must be prepared to build up her trust in him, and this can only be done
over a long period of time. He owes it to her not to expect or
demand a confidence in him which he has not given her time
to regain. It is sometimes difficult, even for the best of wives,
to feel entire confidence in a husband once her confidence in
him has been destroyed. But if he is prepared to be patient
and to work hard to give her back her trust in him, then she
in her turn can make herself trust him accordingly.

A husband or wife may well feel a sense of responsibility
for the other person involved. This is a right feeling, for we
cannot just abandon other people as though they had ceased
to exist. But one thing is certain. The involved partner cannot, even for a single moment, personally look after the person
with whom he has been involved; he must leave that to someone else. Here the counsellor can help, for he can undertake
to see that the other person is cared for and not left friendless,
no one's responsibility. He may well be involved in a counselling situation with the other person. If he is, he must beware
of talking as though there has been nothing good in the
relationship, and all is lost and wasted. There is bound to

have been some good in it, something worth having. (The counsellor may well sort out the wheat from the chaff here.) What has been of value is not waste, and what has been found good and precious must now be sought in other ways, in other places, and in other relationships.

6

Prevention of Breakdown

Our Society More Interested in Cure than Prevention

The society in which we live is more concerned with cure than with prevention. This is not the place to argue this statement; anyone who wishes can verify the truth of it for himself simply by assessing how much time and money we spend on dealing with social breakdowns of one kind or another and how much on trying to prevent such breakdowns happening. One or two illustrations will be sufficient. It costs £700 a year to keep one boy in an Approved School or in Borstal, but let any voluntary community worker try to get as much as that a year for preventive work, for a hundred boys in a youth club, for research into the stresses in society that cause breakdown, and he will soon discover that society is not really concerned in preventing trouble. If a voluntary organization sets out to run a home ("hostel" to use official language) for boys from an Approved School or young men from prison, who have no home of their own or an unsatisfactory home, and if the aim of such an organization is to give such background and support as to help the boys not to get into further trouble, then the Home Office may make a grant towards such a project of up to £100 a year for each boy. This seems to demonstrate that our society thinks it worth spending seven times as much money on dealing with the consequences of social breakdown as in trying to prevent such a breakdown happening.

I have recently been involved in looking after a young girl of seventeen who has left home because of trouble there (not

6

of her making) and who is trying to live on her own. It is almost impossible for a girl of this age to manage on her own without any support of any kind at all. She cannot really earn enough to keep going, she is not old enough to accept the responsibility of living on her own, and the statutory services, bound by their terms of reference, can do next to nothing to help her. I have found myself thinking that it would be so much easier if she were to get into some kind of trouble. If she were to become pregnant or be involved in shoplifting, for example, at once all the statutory social services would sweep into action and she would then have all the support, help, and care that she needed. Because she is making a desperate effort to keep out of trouble nothing, apparently, can be done to help her. Clear proof that our society cares more about cure than prevention.

Social Breakdown and the Community

By "social breakdown" let us understand here any kind of breakdown with an environmental factor, whether the breakdown be delinquency, violence, mental breakdown, marriage breakdown, or anything else that society finds unacceptable. It then appears that another characteristic of our society is that, after having spent its time and money on dealing with the consequence of a social breakdown, it sends the individuals concerned back into the same community and environment in which they broke down before. It might be truer to say "which *caused* them to break down before". It is as though a man were to have in his house a shelf on which he kept some of his most precious pieces of china. Every now and then the vibration caused by the passing traffic would make a piece fall off the shelf and break. He would immediately take it to be expertly repaired and would spare no expense in having it restored as nearly as possible to its original condition. He would then take it home and put it back on the shelf from which it had fallen before, without it ever occurring to him that what he ought to do was to put it on another shelf.

The Community and Marriage Breakdown

In relation to marriage breakdown, we might ask how much time and money we as a society spend on dealing with the consequences of marriage breakdown. (These will include not only counselling but legal proceedings, statutory care for the children, and the care of those involved who suffer some damage or other to their personalities or social well-being.) Compare this with the amount we spend on the prevention of breakdown. What, in fact, are we doing by way of prevention of breakdown apart from organizing marriage preparation courses for engaged couples and discussions on personal relationships for teenagers?

Some research is being done and some articles written about stress in community living, but these are usually about society in general and the writing and reading of them is usually a convenient form of escape from doing anything practical about our own neighbourhood in particular.

The Church Engagé

The French have a word for it, *engagé*, which means both involved and committed in action. It is fashionable nowadays to use such words as "involved" and "committed". It is not always easy to see much action on the part of those who are using them. Here the Church has an opportunity and therefore by definition the responsibility for taking a lead in the local community in which it finds itself. Its job will be to discover the stresses and strains in its immediate neighbourhood which make for breakdown and then to see what as a part of the community it can do to lessen those strains. The Church will not set out to discover the community's need by organizing itself into discussion groups and sitting around talking. Christians are prone to think that they are somehow coming to grips with a situation if they have an earnest discussion about it. The truth is that they are probably not coming to grips with it even mentally, let alone practically, for they probably do not know in truth what the situation is. To know that, Christians must go out into their immediate neighbourhood and find out something about it. They must in fact do a survey. They must discover by active enquiry and questioning what the real needs of the community are. They must come into direct contact with those needs and not meet them at one or two removes by reading about them or by hearing someone talk about them.

The common experience of those who engage in such an activity is first that they discover stress and uncover need of which they would never have thought in a multiplicity of discussions. Then, looking back, they think how obvious was the need they have unearthed. At the same time they realize that they would never have seen it if they had not gone out on a survey and discovered it.

As an illustration of this it may be worth quoting the experience of an Anglican Church and a Methodist Church who were together concerned to discover in their own neighbourhood the difficulties met by women who were bringing up a family on their own—widows, for example, and those who were separated or divorced. They began with two sessions in which they invited experts to talk over with them the problem in general, then they tried to assess what they would find in their own neighbourhood, and finally, after only two training sessions (Christians are apt to demand longer training as a honourable way of postponing action), they went out to interview all those who came within their terms of reference, their names and addresses having previously been ascertained. The results were illuminating. At the outset they had to abandon their original plan of thinking of widows, divorced, and separated as forming one group with common problems; the difficulties of the divorced and separated are altogether different from those of widows. (Any social worker could have told them this at the beginning, but most of us do not take things in until we discover them for ourselves.) Then they came into contact with desperate need of all kinds and hardships in their own streets which they never imagined to exist.

Finally, they found that when in need of advice or support or counselling the people concerned did not know where or to whom to go. Most would go, whatever their need, to the Ministry of Social Security. (The National Assistance Board at the time of the Survey.) It may hurt the local clergy and social workers to know that people do not usually think of turning to them; whether it hurts or not, it is the truth. The first need of the neighbourhood, therefore, became apparent, that there should be some recognized local centre to which people could turn for advice and help, whatever their problems, and somewhere that they would look to for support and care.

In using the word "survey" in this chapter (a popular enough word at the present time) we must notice that most people use it in the sense of outsiders going into a locality and looking at it, or taking a particular field of study and looking into it, and then producing a report on what they have found. They never become involved in the community or concern which is the object of their survey, still less are they committed to any personal action as the result of it. It is clear that the word "survey" is not used in that sense here. It is used here to denote a study of the stress and distress in the community with a view to becoming more involved in that community and more committed to action in it—to becoming *engagé*. The two churches mentioned above, for example, are now committed as a preliminary to establishing a Neighbourhood Citizens Advice Bureau, the kind of centre which their survey revealed to be a first need of the neighbourhood.

Would it not be in the long run a time-saving operation, to put the least value upon it, if the local church, which in word, at any rate, is concerned with married and family life in its own area, were to devote some of the time which it now spends in remedial work to discovering the local community stress that is causing the breakdown and making the remedial work necessary? Does not the same thing apply to all social workers engaged in remedial work in a particular neighbourhood? If all of us who are engaged in counselling, for example, were to give some of our time to discovering for ourselves, not by reading but by personal enquiry and contact, those pressures in our local community which are making our counselling necessary, and were then to give more of our time in action to reduce those pressures, how much misery and degradation might we not prevent?

How isolated, for instance, do young couples feel in a particular neighbourhood? Do they have any real contact and relationship with other families? Are they able to go out together or does the cost and difficulty of finding sitters-in keep them housebound or permit them to go out only separately? What effect does the virtual elimination of the extended family have? (Parents and grandparents no longer live down the road nor are uncles and aunts and cousins just round the corner.) Does a young couple have any sense of belonging to a supporting community or any sense of security in personal friendships? What stress is caused by life in an anonymous society and what effect does this have upon a marriage?

We have lost the warmth in human relationships that comes from living together in a small village community or neighbourhood. It is valueless merely to deplore the loss and do nothing about it. It is equally valueless to set one's sights nostalgically at the re-creation of village life. It is singularly profitless to decry the values of village life, to deny the warmth, and to pretend that whatever there was in village life then we are better off without it. This is just another form of escapism, although a more sophisticated one. It is, surely, more constructive to recognize the values of life in a small, stable, belonging community and by experiment to try to develop those values in our urban communities. No one but a fool will minimize the difficulties, but it is realistic to recognize that the stress caused by life in our present-day urban society produces social breakdown of all kinds and that the time is ripe for local people to try to change some of the conditions of their local community.

The Christians in the locality have an opportunity of giving a lead to the locality. The pitfall to be avoided is the attempt to do everything for everyone. The Church will be doing some good if it tries, out of goodness of heart but with an imperfect conception of service, to do everything for people instead of enabling them to do what needs to be done themselves; but in fact it will be doing far less than the best for people in the neighbourhood. It is less of an achievement to solve the problem of isolation for this or that couple than to enable the different couples to solve their problems among themselves as a group with a common concern for a common neighbourhood need. When people do something like this together, a community warmth is created which cannot be purveyed from the outside however close to the group the purveyors may stand.

The Church as a Belonging and Accepting Community

Besides giving a lead in enabling the local community to discover causes of stress and breakdown within itself and to take action to remove them (creating community warmth in so doing) the Church can see to it that it is itself a warm, belonging, and accepting communion. If it is to be the true Church it *must* do this. This in no way contradicts what has been said above. It is true that it does not seem to be the vocation of the Church at the present time to be a communion set over against the community; it is likely that its present opportunity is to enable the local community to evolve in its urban setting those village-community-type values which make for less stressful living. But this is not going to be achieved in a short time, nor even in the foreseeable future. Because of this and because of its own nature, the Church's vocation also is to be able to offer that warmth, sense of belonging, and acceptance which cannot be found by the majority of people in most of our urban communities. The Church ought to be offering that. Is it? Is the local church as we know it a truly accepting fellowship, in which we accept one another as we are, bear the worst of and make the best of each other as we are? Do we give people a deep sense of belonging and security in belonging? Do members of the fellowship feel that other members as of right can expect from them support on all levels of living and that they in their turn can look for it to others? Or do we reject the difficult person, disgorge the misfit, fail to give a sense of security in belonging, freeze anyone seeking warmth in relationship, and even give the impression that support may be given of grace but cannot be expected as of right?

In theory we may be an accepting and belonging fellowship, but what are the facts? How many "odd persons out" have found a permanent niche in our fellowship? How many who were once delinquents, prisoners, prostitutes, homosexuals? It is no defence for us to say "We have on many occasions offered fellowship to people like this but they never stay with us for long". What have we got to offer except a socially conformist fellowship, even if it is worthy of the name "fellowship", which it often is not? The offer we make in the terms that we make it is seldom more than a futile, meaningless gesture, a drug to lull our consciences into unawareness and to keep us in ignorance of the truth about ourselves as a Christian community. Why do society's casualties not stay with us? Why is it that the social nonconformist cannot find a niche in our fellowship? Is it not time that the local church so re-structured itself that anyone, however awkward and socially unacceptable, could experience in its togetherness a sense of acceptance, belonging, and warmth?

These considerations are relevant in a book on Marriage Counselling for several reasons. It is for the local church to consider whether it is caring for the divorced and separated in any real way. To how many does the church communicate a welcome, not just initially by word, but continually by action which communicates a continuing welcome? How many does it make feel entirely at home? Divorced and separated women suffer greatly. In addition to the difficulties experienced by widows in living alone or in bringing up a family alone, the divorced or separated woman feels the cold shoulder of the community. The community puts them into a separate category. They are not quite respectable; they may be dangerous; it is better to be careful about making friends with them; they are social outsiders. If anyone thinks this attitude of the community is out of date and no longer exists, then clearly he has not done any investigation of how divorced and separated women live, how they feel, and how other people feel about them.

Of still greater relevance to our present purpose is the consideration of what the local church is doing to give support to those who are married, and amongst these, especially those whose marriage is in danger. We have already thought of community stress as a factor in marriage breakdown and we have considered what the Church might be doing about it. This we might call general background preventive work. More particular preventive work is the support of those whose marriage is imperilled. When dealing with a couple whose marriage has broken down, how often does a counsellor feel that with support of the kind we have outlined in this chapter, matters would never have reached breaking point. Indeed, we often feel that with this kind of support the marriage would not only have survived but have done much better than merely survive. But the nearer a marriage comes to breaking point, the less likely it is that the couple will receive support from the local church. For the nearer their marriage is to failure, the nearer they are to being the problem people, the awkward and difficult ones, the social misfits, whom the conforming community tends to eject. The local church will certainly get rid of them unless it is in truth and not only in word *engagé*.

7

The Christian Counsellor

It must not be supposed that a man who is a Christian is necessarily a better counsellor than a man who is not. If his principles and technique of counselling are poorer and his understanding of personality is less, although he is a Christian he may be a worse counsellor. The Christian Faith is no more a substitute for good counselling technique than it is in the medical field for a knowledge of antibiotics. But granted a parity of technique in counselling and understanding of personality, then, I believe, the Christian counsellor has something more to offer. Perhaps it is better not to say "something more" but "something different", for what the Christian has to offer is not an "extra", an "embellishment", a kind of "de luxe model" in counselling, but the grace of God in Christ, and this is something different.

In almost every sphere of life it is good to begin by asking what a thing is and what it is for. The Christian counsellor, before embarking on marriage counselling, would do well to give some thought to answering the questions, "What is marriage?" and, "What is marriage for?" Answering these questions is what is meant for the Christian by "the theology of Marriage".

Theology of Marriage

What is marriage and what is marriage for? What, in other words, is the purpose of marriage in the mind of God? For the traditional answers given to these questions and the history of how they have been arrived at and applied, the standard book to read is *Marriage in Church and State*.[1] To summarize briefly. Marriage is a natural institution, indissoluble except by death; it is effected by contract and completed by consummation; it is not a continuing contract, subject to revision, the contract being to effect the marriage.

According to Lacey, "Marriage ... is a natural necessity. The continuance of the species requires a certain association of man and woman. For the mere begetting of children, a merely passing union would suffice; but more is required. The child requires close attention and long continual care. ... Unlike other animals, man gives birth to fresh offspring while those already born are still dependent on the parents. It follows that a temporary union ... will not suffice; child-bearing goes on for several years, while the firstborn and others are slowly growing to maturity. The connection of the parents, therefore, is indefinitely prolonged, extending even beyond the age of child-bearing. There results a community of interests, an interlacing of habits. As a consequence of this prolonged intimacy there appears the singular phenomenon of human love. ... In a word, the human species is naturally constituted in families."

"Marriage", Lacey continues, "is nothing else but this permanent connection of man and woman for the purpose of producing and raising children." In the words of the 1662 Prayer Book, "First, it was ordained for the procreation of children."

The Christian revelation, according to Lacey, enables us to understand marriage. "The Christian revelation throws new light on the social order of humanity. ... The divine law of marriage is nothing else but the order of nature. Revelation does but enable us to understand it more perfectly."

"Marriage", Lacey goes on, "is an entire union of man and woman". And this is for the sake of the children. "A partial union", he says, "directed exclusively to the business of raising children and allowing the separation of men and women

[1] By T. A. Lacey (S.P.C.K., 1912; revised R. C. Mortimer, 1947).

in regard to other interests, may suffice for the material needs of the children ... but the moral influence of one parent is inevitably weakened, and the full purpose of guardianship is not attained. This can be achieved only when the parties to the union enter fully and unreservedly into one another's lives, or rather into a new joint life which they share on equal terms. ... This close union ... has the further consequence of engendering a new kind of natural affection. ... Indeed there is here found a secondary cause for the divine institution of marriage. 'It was ordained for the mutual society, help, and comfort, that the one ought to have of the other, both in prosperity and adversity.' A marriage unfruitful in children may thus find a place in the economy of nature."

Between baptized Christians marriage is a sacrament which, says Lacey, "is the natural institution raised to a supernatural potency for the conveyance of divine grace delivering man from the fire of concupiscence and producing chastity of soul and body". As the Book of Common Prayer of 1662 has it, "It was ordained for a remedy against sin, and to avoid fornication; that such persons as have not the gift of continency might marry, and keep themselves undefiled members of Christ's body." "As a rule", says Lacey, "in all other animals the sexual act is strictly controlled by the course of nature, and directed to the end of propagation. Concupiscence would therefore seem to be one of the consequences of human freedom. Man has risen above the environment of irresistible conduct, to live under a moral law which he can defy. ... There is thus given by marriage grace to extinguish the flames of concupiscence. Those whom God calls to the exceptional state of virginity receive the special grace of continence; to the rest of mankind is proposed the ordinary grace of marriage, directed to the same end, the production of the supernatural virtue of chaste living. By reason of its sacramental efficacy, marriage is not less chaste than virginity."

I have quoted Lacey at length because his is the classic statement of the traditional Christian view of marriage. But the world of *Marriage in Church and State* is a different world from the one in which we are now living, and a strange world it seems to us. This is not to say that it is a better or worse one, but simply that it is a different one, and its thought-forms are not those of the present day.

If we begin with the teaching of our Lord, we shall come to that teaching with minds differently conditioned from those of another generation. No one can come to the teaching of Christ with a mind blank and unaffected by environment and experience. With our present-day emphasis upon personal relationships we shall pick up every signal, however faint, that seems to speak of relationship in marriage; at the same time we shall fail to respond to signals which someone of Lacey's world would have no difficulty in receiving.

In Mark 10 Christ refers us to the book of Genesis for a consideration of the nature and purpose of marriage in the mind of God, "in the beginning". If we turn to Genesis and look up the context of the words our Lord quotes, we find there no reference at all to the procreation of children but we do find something about relationship: "And the Lord God said, It is not good that the man should be alone; I will make an help meet for him . . . And Adam said, This is now bone of my bones and flesh of my flesh . . . Therefore shall a man leave his father and his mother and shall cleave unto his wife: and they shall be one flesh."

It may be worth noticing that in the references to marriage in the New Testament there is nothing at all said about the procreation of children. This is, perhaps, not very significant, for the references are incidental and do not constitute a treatise on the theology of marriage. It is the traditional Christian view, expressed in the words of the Prayer Book, that marriage was ordained "First, for the procreation of children", but there is nothing in the New Testament or in the Old Testament passage to which our Lord refers us to support that priority.

It is more in keeping with present thinking and experience to say that marriage is commitment in a relationship expressed sexually which normally results in the procreation of children. We might make the equation: Commitment in relationship + Sex = Marriage. "Contract" is too frigid a word and quite inadequate to describe commitment in relationship, but will be included in it; and whereas, in Lacey's view, the contract is not a continuing one, the commitment in relationship certainly is continuing.

Thinking of marriage as a relationship expressed sexually, normally resulting in the procreation of children, makes sense, as the traditional view does not, of a childless marriage and of the continuance of a marriage after the children have ceased to be dependent on their parents. If marriage is "first for the procreation of children" and only then does "this close union . . . have the further consequence of engendering a new kind of affection . . ." it is hard to see the reason for the continuance of marriage for what Lacey calls the "secondary" cause when the first has not or is not being fulfilled.

The relationship in marriage is prior in essence and in time to the procreation of children and it makes a difference if we think of it so. Perhaps the Introduction to the Marriage Service of the Book of Common Prayer could be re-written in some such way as follows: "Matrimony was ordained to be the commitment of a man and woman to each other in a life-long exclusive relationship expressed in bodily love; from which expression there is normally the procreation of children. It was ordained that in this relationship one ought to have of the other society, help, and comfort, both in prosperity and adversity."

If it be asked why, if the relationship is prior, in heaven "men and women do not marry" (Mark 12.25), the answer is that the relationship of person and person in that life is not expressed in bodily love and therefore is not exclusive and has no need to be so.

Divorce

The Christian counsellor must also consider his attitude towards divorce. Sometimes he will be asked, "Do you think I should divorce him?"; sometimes he will be told, "I'm going to get a divorce"; and sometimes, "I want to get married in church, but I've been divorced; what is the position?"

The Church of England does not in any circumstances countenance the Church's Marriage Service being used for a divorced person during the lifetime of his or her former partner. A clergyman of the Established Church has by civil law the right to conduct the marriage of a divorced person if he wishes, though no incumbent can be compelled to lend his church for the purpose; but against this is the regulation of the Convocation of Canterbury made in 1957 that "the Church should not allow the use of that Service [the Marriage Service] in the case of anyone who has a former partner still living". Though no bishop would have redress against any clergyman who followed the civil law rather than the ecclesiastical regulation, nevertheless the mind of the Church is quite clear for those who wish to be loyal to it, and in practice, with only a very occasional exception, it is the ecclesiastical regulation which is followed. No public Service is to be held for those who have contracted a civil marriage after divorce. The saying of private prayers by the Minister with the couple concerned is neither enjoined nor forbidden. (For the Resolutions of the Convocations see the Appendix.)

The attitude of the Church of Rome is the same, but that Church has a number of escape clauses. It is prepared to nullify a marriage in far more instances than the Church of England is prepared to do so. (Nullity is the declaration that a marriage "never was" and therefore that the couple are as free to marry whom they will as any other single persons. The Church of England does not itself nullify a marriage but accepts the decrees of nullity of the civil authority.)

The Orthodox Church allows divorce and remarriage after

divorce for certain causes, including adultery, desertion, banishment, treason, attempted murder of one party by the other, and insanity.

The Free Churches in England will marry a divorced person, but not everyone who asks. In the Baptist, Congregational, Methodist, and Presbyterian Churches the decision is left to the local Minister (the Methodist would normally discuss the matter with his Chairman of District). The local Minister goes into the matter thoroughly and has his own criteria for deciding whether or not the couple in question should have their marriage solemnized in church. In practice, between one-third and one-half of those who apply are allowed to be married in church.

If we begin by thinking of the traditional theology of marriage and stop there, we shall conclude that man cannot put asunder what God has joined together. If marriage is a "natural institution" and "indissoluble except by death", as Lacey says, then it cannot be dissolved except by death for anyone, whether Christian or not and whether solemnized in church or not.

If, on the other hand, we consider our own pastoral experience we shall come to a different conclusion. Much more often than we like for our peace of mind, we are in contact with someone whose marriage has broken down, and, as far as human judgement can see, has broken down beyond any rational prospect of repair. In such circumstances it is hard to say that a client is wrong to want to start again with another partner and to expect help and support from the Church in doing so.

Simply to say that the Church is in a dilemma does no sort of justice to that dilemma. The Church is in a situation which without any exaggeration may be termed impossible. The Report of the Joint Committee of Convocations in 1956, on which the 1957 regulations are based, together with the ensuing debate, needs only to be read for the complexity of the problem and the Church's perplexity with regard to it to be appreciated. There is, on the one hand, the right desire and the moral obligation to uphold Christ's standard of marriage and, on the other, the genuine desire to care pastorally for those who have suffered a marriage breakdown.

A situation with which I am faced at this moment, of the kind that every parish priest knows, illustrates the difficulty: A young woman in her twenties is making a courageous and sometimes desperate effort to bring up a child on her own because her husband, after behaving towards her with cruelty and callousness, left her within a year of their marriage; attempts to make contact with him have proved unavailing. Other circumstances make it as near certain as possible that they will not live together again. Am I to conclude that this young woman, apparently not called to the single state but meant by God and therefore constituted by him to live in an intimate, affectionate, supporting relationship with a husband should now and for, perhaps, the next fifty years be denied the opportunity of doing so?

The young woman is a regular communicant and makes a great effort to be at the Parish Communion with her child every Sunday. Should she ever come to me and ask if she can be married in church I shall have to say to her in obedience to the regulations of the Convocations, "I cannot marry you in church, but if you go to the Registry Office and are married there, you can come to church afterwards together with your husband and I can say some prayers with you." If she asks about making her communion, I must refer the matter to the Bishop. The regulations about the admission to communion of those who have been married again with a previous partner still living may vary from diocese to diocese, but most Bishops will ask that someone who is an active communicant at the time of entering upon a second marriage should attend church regularly for a period, perhaps twelve months, but without receiving the Sacrament. This renunciation is to be seen as an offering to God in reparation and as an earnest sign of serious intention to resume communicant life when the Bishop gives permission.

Some may say, "If this young woman were truly a committed Christian she would not want to get married again and God would give her grace to live on her own for the rest of her life." God will certainly give her grace to do all that he wants her to do. Are we entitled to conclude that whatever the circumstances, God will want a young woman in her situation to remain as she is until her marriage is dissolved by death?

The teaching of our Lord seems quite clear. "The question was put to him. Is it lawful for a man to divorce his wife? He asked in return, What did Moses command you? They answered, Moses permitted a man to divorce his wife by note of dismissal. Jesus said to them It was because you were so unteachable that he made this rule for you; but in the beginning, at the creation, God made them male and female. For this reason a man shall leave his father and his mother and be made one with his wife; and two shall become one flesh. It follows that they are no longer two individuals; they are one flesh. What God has joined together, man must not separate. When they were indoors again the disciples questioned him about this matter; he said to them, Whoever divorces his wife and marries another commits adultery against her; so too, if she divorces her husband and marries another, she commits adultery. (Mark 10.2–12. See also Luke 16.18. Most Commentators agree that the exceptive clause of Matthew 5 and 19 are not the words of Christ; in any case there is no agreement as to what they mean.)

And St Paul writes: "To the married I give this ruling, which is not mine but the Lord's: a wife must not separate herself from her husband; if she does, she must either remain unmarried or be reconciled to her husband; and the husband must not divorce his wife" (1 Cor. 7.10–11).

Some say that Christ is not here giving us a rule to be applied with literal meaning in all circumstances, but that he is showing us the mind of God for a man and a woman, the perfection in marriage on which we must set our gaze and towards which we must strive. They point out that it is unlike Christ and his way of dealing with us, as we know him elsewhere in the Gospels, to lay down a law for us. They conclude, therefore, that he is not here establishing a law but a principle.

Others point out that the reaction of the disciples to the Lord's teaching, "If that is the position with husband and wife, it is better to refrain from marriage" presupposes something hard and challenging in that teaching.

Starting from the existential pastoral situation and working from there, it must often seem to the parish priest that the Church of England, in its attitude towards marriage and divorce is not so much wrong as not *right* enough! The Church has two obligations. It must, on the one hand, not only by its word but by its action make clear the teaching of Christ that marriage is meant to be a lifelong relationship, and, on the other, give every help and support to those who have suffered a marriage breakdown, want to start afresh with another partner, and sincerely mean to do better than before. The Church of England fulfils the first of these obligations admirably, but the second not so well. The Free Churches better fulfil the obligations of pastoral care, but it may be said that their present practice of marrying divorced persons obscures the teaching of Christ. The Roman Catholic Church with its declarations of nullity seems to call a spade a trowel! It may be thought that if the Church of England were to adopt, with modifications, the practice of the Orthodox Church, which solemnizes the marriage of divorced persons but with a difference in the Service, which is adapted to the circumstances, then it would be acting with greater pastoral wisdom and still pointing as clearly to the teaching of Christ.

Such action would need theological as well as pastoral justification. Is this possible along something like the following lines? A man and a woman were created by God "in the beginning" to live in a perfect, lifelong relationship. Anything else is now less than that perfection to which God calls us all in every part of our lives. "You must therefore be all goodness, just as your heavenly father is all good", we are told, and therefore the goodness of God must be the aim of all of us. But we all fall short of that goodness, some in one way, some in another. We have to put up with less than the best both in ourselves and in others. We frequently have to make the best of a bad job, recognizing that, while it is a bad job, it is nevertheless the best that is possible in the circumstances. This is the only way in which we can live and accept ourselves and others; it is the way in which God accepts us too. We are frequently confronted with situations, brought about by human folly or wickedness, in which we have to choose between two evils, and the only reason why one is not evil for us and the other is, is that it is the better way of the two; it is not absolute but relative good. We are frequently, too, meeting in our own lives and in the lives of others examples of God's will being thwarted and made impossible of achievement. A typical example is that of a young man whose vocation was to be a surgeon, so injured in a car accident, entirely the result of human selfishness, that his vocation was made impossible of fulfilment. Yet God can bear the worst of the situation and make the best of it.

A man and a woman are called by God to live in a perfect, lifelong relationship. (We must not overlook the fact that the relationship is meant to be a perfect one; often we talk as though the final break is the imperfection that matters and ignore all the imperfections that have led up to it.) Through sin, ignorance, and hardness of heart in themselves (and perhaps in other people) they have come to the point where their own persons and their relationship are in such a state that they cannot fulfil God's purpose for them; their marriage has broken down beyond repair. They have put themselves asunder. (It is the two persons concerned, not the presiding judge, who puts them asunder. The judge pronounces what the situation is.) Yet they were each made for living in the intimate, supporting relationship of marriage and cannot be expected not to do so; their vocation is to marriage and not to celibacy.

At this point we must ask what the relationship of the remarried person is both with his former partner and with his new. Would the former relationship be dissolved or would the Church, interpreting the words of Christ literally, be giving a man a licence to live in adultery?

There is some part of a man's relationship with his former partner that is not dissolved and cannot be. We cannot enter into a deep, intimate relationship with someone and then leave that person and relationship behind as though they had never existed. We leave some part of ourselves behind with them and there is something of them left in us. St Paul applies the words of Genesis "They twain shall be one flesh" to being linked with a harlot (1 Cor. 6.16). We cannot have a relationship with a harlot and come out of it unaffected. Entering into the intimate relationship of being "one flesh" with her makes its mark upon us and we can never be as though it had not happened. This is bound to affect any subsequent relationship that we may enter into, for we come to that relationship a different person.

This is true, of course, of all relationships. They all make their mark on us for better or worse, and we are different people because of them. How much more does this apply to the relationship of marriage, in which each has been so committed and so close as to be each other's next of kin. It is only the person that a man in fact is that can enter into a relationship with someone. He cannot continually wipe the slate clean of past experiences. He cannot expunge entirely the experience of a former marriage. If he bears on his personality the deep impressions made by one relationship in marriage, then it as the person affected by those that he comes to another:

> Our past deeds follow with us from afar,
> And what we have been makes us what we are.

Is a remarried divorced person living in adultery? The word "adultery" has heavy emotional overtones and usually implies for us a very sinful sexual relationship from which every good man would shrink with horror and which ought to be ended forthwith. If there is any truth in what is said above, then we ought not to recoil with horror at the thought of remarriage after divorce. If we think of such a relationship as a less than ideal one, but one which may or may not be sinful according to the circumstances, and cease to think of it in terms of whether or not it is adulterous, we may be less inclined to distribute blame. In any case, when considering the word "adultery" and attempting to understand what our Lord meant in applying it to remarriage, we must remember how conditioned we are to reacting with very strong emotions to its application to a relationship. It is worth recalling that Christ said, "If a man looks on a woman with a lustful eye, he has already committed adultery with her in his heart." Some would say that *in this sense* very many happily married, godly men have committed adultery.

Does the attitude towards the marriage relationship, divorce, and remarriage outlined above adequately uphold the teaching of Christ or does it, as in the parable of the Unjust Steward, lower the master's demands? In another parable a servant released from his debt catches hold of the throat of a fellow servant to extract the last penny due, not an attitude that receives the Lord's commendation. Let us recognize one thing, that there is much we do not know about the nature of human relationships, whether the relationships of marriage or any other. We cannot explain them precisely or adequately. They are, like the relationship of Christ and his Church, "great mysteries".

One thing, however, seems clear: we have no right to insist that a divorced person should not remarry unless we, as members of the Church, undergo a radical reformation with regard to our fellowship. A man or woman living without a partner, perhaps trying in the face of all the odds (our society does precious little to help them) to bring up a family, has every right to expect from us, if we bid them remain un-married, the ultimate in the way of warmth, affection, friend-ship, care, and support. The individual has every right to expect his local church to be his family, filling the emptiness with affection, banishing the loneliness with friendship, sup-porting the weakness with strength. I wonder how many

churches, even of those known for the strength of their fellowship, are doing this in any effective way, and how many are
like one church I know, which a separated woman has
attended now for over a year. Not once has she been invited
into anyone's home, no one has made any effort to make
friends with her; if she wants a small job done of the sort that
a husband would ordinarily do, she has to employ the local
odd-job man. Unless the local church, in effective action as
well as in word, is prepared to be the true family of those who
are separated or divorced it has no right to expect them to
remain unmarried. To teach and not to act is not only to be
like the Pharisees who "make up heavy packs and pile them
on men's shoulders but will not raise a finger to lift the load
themselves", but is also to keep up with the Pilates in the
matter of hand washing.

Should a counsellor ever suggest separation or divorce to a
client? I certainly think it right on occasions to make the
suggestion of a separation. There are certain things which no
woman should be expected to put up with from a man, or a
man from a woman; for example, cruelty, terrorizing, callousness, utter neglect, persistent infidelity. I am, of course, thinking of severe forms of these and not minor occasional occur-
rences. It is not holy love to put up with everything uncom-
plainingly. It is probably not good for the husband, let us
say, if his wife accepts without effective protest whatever
treatment he chooses to mete out to her. Certainly it is not
good for their marriage. Separation may be the only safe
course for a partner to take. Sometimes it may be therapeutic.

I do not, however, think that I could ever suggest divorce to
anyone nor give them wholehearted encouragement if the
suggestion had occurred to them already. Divorce is such an
irrevocable step, its consequences so great that here, above
all, it is necessary to be non-directive. At the same time, if
someone's mind were set upon divorce, I would not, I hope,
in view of all such a decision means, try to persuade them into
another course of action. I conceive it to be my part as a
counsellor to help a client to sort out and to see all that is for

and against a particular course of action, taking everything, including conscience, into account. It is my duty then to stand aside and let the one who is personally involved come to their decision.

"You shall know the Truth and the Truth shall set you free"

Truth, like charity, begins at home. Knowing the truth about ourselves is the beginning of knowing the truth about other people. Knowledge of the stresses and anxieties in ourselves will help us to understand what other people are talking about when they are speaking of themselves; it will help us to pick up stray hints and signs and make articulate something that a client is saying to us.

Our Lord said, "You shall know the truth and the truth shall set you free." We are the prisoners of our own interior stresses; we cannot be free of them until we know the truth about them. But knowing the truth about them is not enough; we also need to know the truth about Christ and how he deals with our anxieties and stress and sets us free from them.

It is only as we know our inner torture that we can experience the power of Christ in dealing with it. "My grace is all you need; power comes to its full strength in weakness," he says to us (2 Cor. 12.9). We can only speak with conviction of how the power of Christ can release a man from his personality problems if we have first felt him release us from our own.

Into the Pain

We all want to escape from the pain and torment of a situation, and this is what we often do: we all have our own ways of escape. These enable us to go on living and are often helpful, providing that we do not rely upon them entirely. Getting away from the pain relieves the pressure on us for a time, but this is negative and does nothing to deal with whatever is

THE CHRISTIAN COUNSELLOR 97

causing the pressure. Very often the most positive way out of
the pain is to go right into it. Here in the depth of the pain
we find Christ, and not only Christ but Christ crucified,
touching us with his own experience at the very point where
we are most hurt. Inside we feel alone, forsaken, weak; Christ
crucified touches us with his own experience of aloneness, for-
sakenness, and weakness. Inside everyone, underneath the
surface, in the depths, there is a hell of pain. If instead of
running away from it we run into it, we find Christ in it.
(This is one application of "he descended into hell", when we
find he has descended into the hell within us.) Christ adheres
to us at the point where his experience touches our own, rises
from the deadness within us, and in rising takes us with him
to a new life freed from the bondage of death within.

If we have known this ourselves, then our experience will
be of value when we are trying to help some of the people who
come to us and of whom we have spoken in earlier chapters.
The homosexual, for example, finds the attempts to form a
relationship with a woman unbearable. If he can, for once,
cease running from the agony, escaping from it in relationships with men, if he can instead descend into the pain, he
can hope that Christ will raise him out of it to new life. This
is far from easy, but experience shows that it is possible.

Christ and Quarrelling

In counselling those who quarrel and fly into violent tempers,
it is wise to remember that those who are most anxious to
keep even-tempered and are making desperate attempts to do
so often fail through trying too hard. It is glorious, when
someone says, "I try so hard", to see the effect of replying, "I
suggest that you give up trying". Often we try so hard ourselves that we do not allow any room for the grace of God to
work within us. When we stop trying and relax in Christ by
faith, then the grace of God can operate.

We can remember, too, that Christ on the cross is bearing
all the frustrations, bitterness, anger, stress, and violence of

the world. Instead of bottling it all up inside us, we can let it out at him. It is useless to try to press it further and further down; that will do no good. It is worse than useless to let it out at wife, husband, or child. The only safe thing to do with our temper is to let it out at Christ, to vent all our spite on him so that he may bear it for us. It is a releasing thing to be able to say "Christ, how I hate you for all the misery and frustration I feel . . . How I hate you for not making things better for me . . . But, Lord, I let this out at you because this is what I know you want me to do; Lord, you are bearing all the temper of the world and you want me to let mine out at you so that you may bear it for me . . . Lord, I know you don't want me to shut it all up inside myself to fester . . . I know you don't want me to let it out at my wife, but at you . . ." Because we let out all our frustrations and temper at Christ it is no longer in us; he has borne it for us, as he wills to do.

In Chapter 4 we saw that it is easier for the person who is more "in the right" in a quarrel to accept the blame and the responsibility. This seems unreasonable, unjust, and unfair. Should, however, the person whom we are counselling be one who is prepared to look at Christ and learn from him, then he has good reason to believe that it is the innocent bearing the blame who restores the relationship.

8

Working with Others

In one sense every priest is a Social Worker and a Community Worker. (To avoid misunderstanding let me add that this is not all, nor yet principally, what I think a clergyman is for. Nevertheless, in so far as he is concerned with human need in his neighbourhood and involved in the community, he is both a Social and Community Worker.) As such he will find himself working with other Social and Community Workers. Sometimes when seeing a particular couple he will find that the local doctor, the Probation Officer, the Children's Officer are also involved. Sometimes a Social Worker will ask for the help of the clergyman, sometimes the clergyman will want the help of one of the statutory or voluntary Social Workers. Sometimes the priest will want to refer someone to the Marriage Guidance Council, sometimes that body will get into touch with the local Minister. No one, of course, will consult any other person without the permission of the client concerned. This is of the utmost importance.

It is important that the parish priest should have some knowledge of, and more than a nodding acquaintance with, the social agencies at work in his locality. In a large city he cannot be expected to know all the agencies thoroughly and all the workers personally; but he will know something about the social services in his town, something of their work. He will know some of the members of the medical profession, some Probation Officers, some Family Case Workers, some Psychiatric Social Workers, enough for him to have an understanding of the world of the full-time Social Workers (it is a distinct world!) to appreciate their training, attitude, and approach. Clergy and Social Workers should know each other well enough to be able to work together in harmony and with respect for each other's values and professions.

The Marriage Guidance Council

The Marriage Guidance Council is a voluntary organization. It depends upon voluntary subscriptions, but the National Marriage Guidance Council receives a Government grant and the local Marriage Guidance Councils, which have a great deal of autonomy, receive Local Authority grants.

The Objectives of the National Marriage Guidance Council are set out as follows:

"The National Marriage Guidance Council is concerned primarily with marriage and family relationships, and believes that the well-being of society is dependent on the stability of marriage. Its Objectives are:

1. To provide a confidential counselling service for people who have difficulties or anxieties in their marriages or in other personal relationships.

2. To provide an education service in personal relationships for young people, engaged or newly married couples, and parents.

3. To equip men and women to do this work by means of a national system of selection, training, tutorial support, and supervision.

4. To publish and distribute literature on a wide variety of topics relating to marriage and family life.

5. To provide courses and conferences for teachers, ministers of religion, youth leaders and others, and to co-operate with workers in related fields."

Selection and Training of Counsellors

The local Marriage Guidance Council, after interviewing

those who volunteer to be counsellors, will, if the candidates are thought suitable, sponsor them to the National Marriage Guidance Council for selection. The candidates then attend two selection conferences organized by the National Marriage Guidance Council and, if then accepted, go forward for training. In response to the question about the personal qualities needed in counsellors the Marriage Guidance Council says, "Speaking generally, we are looking for persons who are kindly, tolerant, and accepting in their personal relationships, but at the same time capable of being objective."

The training course consists of at least four residential periods of forty-eight hours, regular attendances at a counsellors' discussion group, and supervision by a tutor.

How good is the Marriage Guidance Council?

My own experience of the Marriage Guidance Council in Bristol is that it is a very good movement indeed and I have learnt a great deal from its counsellors. Frequently I have referred someone to the Council either for specialist advice or because circumstances made me think that this was the right move. Never have I regretted any referral; always I have been grateful for the help given. Naturally, however, local branches of the Marriage Guidance Council differ in quality and it would be wise to be guided by local knowledge and experience.

The Marriage Guidance Council is quite definitely non-directive, sometimes, I feel, too rigidly so. This is perhaps the only criticism that I have to make of the Marriage Guidance Council—that it is in bondage to its own rules and its counsellors are not free enough to be flexible and to break the rules when, as far as can be seen, the situation demands it.

Clients are always seen at the local Marriage Guidance Council office. A client is never seen at the counsellor's home and the counsellor does not visit the client's home, except in exceptional circumstances, for example, when a partner to the marriage is an invalid and confined to the house. Generally speaking these rules of counselling work very well; I only wish that the Marriage Guidance Council did not stick so rigidly by them. Inflexibility can destroy, or at any rate fail to save.

The Probation Service

Although it is not generally known, the Probation Service acts as a Marriage Counselling agency. When legal aid for matrimonial cases could be obtained only through the Probation Service, in a city the size of Bristol two officers, a man and a woman, were on duty full time seeing the people who came to them with marriage problems of one kind or another. Now that legal aid may be obtained without reference to the Probation Service more people are inclined to go straight to a lawyer. This is probably on balance a loss, because a good probation officer could do much towards effecting a reconciliation before legal proceedings had been initiated or lawyers' letters written. Any citizen has the right to go to the Probation Office with a marriage problem, and even after the recent decline in numbers the Bristol Probation Service sees about a thousand people a year in connection with marriage problems alone.

A probation officer will also be involved in dealing with marriage problems in connection with his probation and after-care work. (The Probation Service is now the statutory authority for the after-care of those coming out of prison, detention centres, Borstal, and Approved Schools.)

Anyone involved in counselling of any kind will sometimes be involved in working with the Probation Service. It is impossible to overstress how important it is that a clergyman should know some officers very well and be on terms of personal friendship with them whenever possible. Many of what I consider to be the happiest, most fruitful and rewarding pieces of work in co-operation with others have been done with probation officers; several officers I count as my personal friends and my respect for them is without limit. Having said that, I am bound to say also that in my experience they seem to suffer from the "*my* case" attitude more than most other Social Workers. This is, of course, an "occupational hazard" of all of us engaged in what are termed the "helping professions". The doctor says "*my* patient", the clergyman "*my* parishioner", the schoolmaster "*my* pupil", the Children's Officer "*my* family". There is this tendency to want others to be hewers of wood and drawers of water but to exclude them from any real work with the person concerned.

The Legal Profession

It happens that a man or woman will come to us to ask how to obtain a divorce or separation. As we have seen, this can sometimes be translated, "I want to ask your help in making my marriage a better marriage and I don't know how to begin but this will do." On the other hand, we are occasionally asked a question which involves some knowledge of the law. If the client seriously wants legal advice or if the matter is one which involves more than a passing acquaintance with the law, then clearly the right thing to do is to refer the client to a lawyer or the Citizens' Advice Bureau. But frequently a rudimentary knowledge of the law, of the kind that a counsellor might be expected to have, is all that is needed to answer a question.

It is valuable if a counsellor knows one or two members of the legal profession whom he can consult unofficially, to satisfy his mind on a point or to ask whether in such and such a situation the client should be advised to see a lawyer.

The Law at Present[1]

It may be useful if I set down here some of the main points

[1] This is the law at the present time (October 1968). Since this and the following sections (*Modifications of the Law in the Future*) were written a Private Member's Bill, called The Divorce Reform Bill, has been presented to Parliament. Whether it will eventually become law and, if so, with what changes, it is impossible to say. Its chief provisions are summarized in Appendix B.

of the law of which a counsellor sometimes needs to be aware:

Three Years' Limitation means that no petition for divorce can be presented within three years of the date of the marriage unless leave to do so is granted by a High Court judge. This is only granted in exceptional circumstances.

Grounds for Divorce are adultery, desertion, cruelty, unsoundness of mind, sodomy, bestiality, and rape.

Desertion must be without cause and for a period of three years. It may be actual or constructive. The party who intends bringing the cohabitation to an end, and whose conduct in reality causes its termination, commits the act of desertion. When constructive desertion is alleged the conduct complained of must be of a serious and convincing nature that would drive away a reasonable partner.

Desertion is precluded as a ground for divorce if it is with the other partner's consent, if it is by a decree of judicial separation, by a justice's order containing a non-cohabitation clause, by resumption of cohabitation, by refusal without cause of a genuine offer to return.

Cruelty is difficult to define, but the conduct alleged must be of a grave kind, wilful, unjustifiable, such as to cause injury to body or mind or give rise to a reasonable fear of such injury.

Unsoundness of mind means that the partner must be incurably of unsound mind and for at least five years immediately before the petition have been continuously under care and treatment.

Sodomy, bestiality, and rape are grounds of divorce available only to the wife. A wife may be guilty of cruelty if she persists in unnatural offences and thereby injures her husband's health.

Absolute Bars to Divorce are failure to prove the offence (even in an undefended suit the court must be satisfied that the case is proved), connivance, condonation, and collusion.

Discretionary Bars to Divorce are unreasonable delay in presenting the petition, adultery by the petitioner, cruelty by the petitioner before the offence complained of; desertion or wilful separation is a bar to a suit based on adultery or cruelty, if it preceded the adultery or cruelty; wilful neglect or misconduct conducive to adultery, desertion, or unsoundness of mind is a bar to a suit based on these grounds.

Presumption of Death may be decreed by the court when there are reasonable grounds for supposing that the other partner to the marriage is dead.

The Grounds for Judicial Separation are the same as those for divorce with the additional grounds of failure to comply with a decree for restitution of conjugal rights and certain other grounds, e.g. a husband's attempted unnatural conduct.

The Effect of a Decree of Judicial Separation is that the parties are married but the duty to cohabit no longer applies. The decree ends if cohabitation is resumed and must be discharged on the application of one of the parties.

A Decree for the Restitution of Conjugal Rights orders return to cohabitation (not necessarily to intercourse); non-compliance by either party is a ground for judicial separation and also enables the court to deal with the custody, education, and maintenance of the children.

A Marriage is Void if there is an already existing marriage, if there is lack of consent (for example, where there is duress, mistake, or fraud as to the identity of the other party or the nature of the ceremony), insanity, if the parties fall within the prohibited degrees of consanguinity and affinity, if either party is under age, if the formalities are defective (this does not usually invalidate a marriage unless both parties act knowingly and wilfully).

A Marriage is Voidable if there is inability to consummate the marriage or wilful refusal to consummate the marriage, if one party at the time of the marriage was of unsound mind, a mental defective, or subject to recurrent fits of insanity or

8

epilepsy, if one party was suffering at the time of the marriage from venereal disease in a communicable form, or if the respondent was at the time of the marriage pregnant by some person other than the petitioner.

Maintenance of wife and children can be ordered by the High Court if the husband neglects to maintain them. The duty of maintenance goes with the duty of cohabitation. If a wife deserts her husband, or if he has just cause for leaving her, he is not liable for her maintenance.

If the wife is the guilty party in a divorce suit, she usually gets no maintenance for herself except sometimes a small compassionate allowance. If both partners are guilty, the husband may be ordered to pay substantial maintenance.

The court can make provision for the maintenance of the children of a marriage or for the child of one party (including an illegitimate or an adopted child) if the child has been accepted by the other party as a member of the family. The general principle is that the children must not be allowed to suffer because of the parents' dispute.

Enforcement of maintenance orders is not always easy, if the husband wishes to avoid his obligations. Sometimes an "attachment of earnings" order may be obtained by which the money is deducted from the husband's earnings at source.

Custody of Children may be provided for by the court and in dealing with this the welfare of the child is the paramount consideration. In practice it is usual for the mother to be given the custody of very young children, whether she is the guilty party or not. Each case is considered on its merits and there is no hard and fast rule about it. Access to the child is usually allowed to the party to whom custody is not granted.

Costs of all proceedings are in the discretion of the court.

Damages may be claimed by a husband against the co-respondent. A wife cannot claim damages from the woman with whom her husband has committed adultery; she may bring a common law action for enticement.

Modification of the Law in the Future

Within a comparatively short time modifications are likely to be made in the law. At the present time it is impossible to make even a tentative forecast of what they will be.

In July 1966 the Report of a Group appointed by the Archbishop of Canterbury in 1964 was published under the title of *Putting Asunder*. The Group proposed that the doctrine of matrimonial offence should not be the basis of a divorce law and that there should be one ground for divorce, the breakdown of the marriage, and the court should make an inquest into the marriage to see if it had broken down irretrievably.

Putting Asunder was referred to the Law Commission and its Report was issued in November 1966.

The Law Commission welcomed the rejection by the Archbishop's Group of exclusive reliance on matrimonial offence, but considered the proposal for a thorough inquest by the court into every marriage that came before it in a divorce case to be procedurally impracticable. While putting forward no definite proposals itself it set out the field of choice as follows:

(a) *Breakdown without inquest.* The court would on proof of a period of separation, and in the absence of evidence to the contrary, assume that the marriage had broken down.

The Commission states as its opinion that if this were to be the sole comprehensive ground of divorce, the period of separation could not be much more than six months. If the period were longer, it would be an intolerable hardship for an innocent party who had been the victim of outrageous conduct and who could under the present law obtain a divorce much more quickly.

(b) *Divorce by Consent.* The Commission says that this would only be practicable as an additional and not as a sole comprehensive ground of divorce, that it would not be more than a palliative and would probably be unacceptable except in the case of marriage where there were no dependent children, and even in these might lead to the dissolution of marriages that had not broken down irretrievably.

(c) *The Separation Ground*. This, the Commission says, would involve introducing as a ground for divorce a period of separation, irrespective of which party was at fault. Since this period would be substantially longer than six months, it would be practicable only as an addition to the existing grounds based on matrimonial offence.

Others Who May be Involved in Helping a Couple

I have written at length about co-operation with the Marriage Guidance Council, the Probation Service, and the Legal Profession and have mentioned briefly the Children's Officers, Family Case Workers, Doctors (this includes psychiatrists, of course) and Psychiatric Social Workers. This is not the place to write comprehensively about the statuory and voluntary social services, but only to state that from experience I find myself involved in working with those already mentioned, together with Medical Social Workers and Moral Welfare Workers (sometimes known by a different name, e.g. Family Welfare Workers) more than with any others.

People who come to us do not like to think that we are passing them around, as though we cannot be bothered to see them and want to hand them on to someone else. Yet we must beware of falling into the "my case" attitude and thinking that no one can help a couple as well as we can. We should be ready to ask others to help, recognize that no one has a monopoly of counselling and helping ability, and that our client may well do better with another person. If our client senses that we are not in a hurry to off-load him on to someone else, nor desperately anxious to keep him to ourselves, if he sees that we know what we are about in calling in other people's help, his confidence in our concern for him and his problem and in our competency is bound to be increased.

APPENDIX A

RESOLUTIONS PASSED BY THE CONVOCATION OF CANTERBURY ON MARRIAGE AND DIVORCE

1

"That this House reaffirms the following four Resolutions of 1938, and in place of Resolution 5 then provisionally adopted by the Upper House substitutes Resolution 2 (A) below, which restates the procedure generally followed since 1938."

1 "That this House affirms that according to God's will, declared by our Lord, marriage is in its true principle a personal union, for better or for worse, of one man with one woman, exclusive of all others on either side, and indissoluble save by death."

2 "That this House also affirms as a consequence that re-marriage after divorce during the lifetime of a former partner always involves a departure from the true principle of marriage as declared by our Lord."

3 "That in order to maintain the principle of lifelong obligation which is inherent in every legally contracted marriage and is expressed in the plainest terms in the Marriage Service, the Church should not allow the use of that Service in the case of anyone who has a former partner still living."

4 "That while affirming its adherence to our Lord's principle and standard of marriage as stated in the first and second of the above resolutions, this House recognizes that the actual discipline of particular Christian communions in this matter has varied widely from time to time and place to place, and holds that the Church of England is competent to enact such a discipline of its own in regard to marriage as may from time to time appear most salutary and efficacious."

2(A)

"Recognizing that the Church's pastoral care for all people includes those who during the lifetime of a former partner contract a second union, this House approves the following pastoral regulations as being the most salutary in present circumstances:

(a) When two persons have contracted a marriage in civil law during the lifetime of a former partner of either of them, and either or both desire to be baptized or confirmed or to partake of the Holy Communion, the incumbent or other priest having the cure of their souls shall refer the case to the Bishop of the diocese, with such information as he has and such recommendations as he may desire to make.

(b) The Bishop in considering the case shall give due weight to the preservation of the Church's witness to our Lord's standard of marriage and to the pastoral care of those who have departed from it.

(c) If the Bishop is satisfied that the parties concerned are in good faith and that their receiving of the Sacraments would be for the good of their souls and ought not to be a cause of offence to the Church, he shall signify his approval thereof both to the priest and to the party or parties concerned: this approval shall be given in writing and shall be accepted as authoritative both in the particular diocese and in all other dioceses of the province."

2(B)

"No public Service shall be held for those who have contracted a civil marriage after divorce. It is not within the competence of the Convocations to lay down what private prayers the curate in the exercise of his pastoral Ministry may say with the persons concerned, or to issue regulations as to where or when these prayers shall be said."

2(C)

"Recognizing that pastoral care may well avert the danger of divorce if it comes into play before legal proceedings have been started, this House urges all clergy in their preparation of couples for marriage to tell them, both for their own sakes and for that of their friends, that the good offices of the clergy are always available."

THE DIVORCE REFORM BILL

The Divorce Reform Bill has not yet been passed by Parliament. It may or may not become law. Its chief provisions may be briefly summarized as follows:

1. There shall be only one ground for divorce, that the marriage has broken down irretrievably.

2. Proof of breakdown shall be one or more of the following facts:

(a) The respondent has committed adultery and the petitioner finds it intolerable to live with the respondent.

(b) The respondent has behaved in such a way that the petitioner cannot reasonably be expected to live with the respondent.

(c) Desertion for a continuous period of two years.

(d) Separation for two years, provided that neither party objects to a decree being granted.

(e) Separation for five years.

3. The court may require evidence that some attempt has been made at reconciliation. The court may adjourn the proceedings to enable an attempt at reconciliation to be made.

4. A decree may be refused if divorce would result in grave financial or other hardship to the respondent. Provision is made for the financial protection of the respondent in certain cases. Provision may also be made for the referral to the court of any financial arrangements made or proposed to provide for either of the parties for any relevant child.

5. The existence of any of the facts mentioned in 2. shall be a ground for the presentation of a petition for judicial separation. In hearing such a petition the court shall not be concerned to consider whether the marriage has broken down irretrievably.

For Further Reading

The National Marriage Guidance Council publishes a list of recommended books and booklets. Its Training Department issues a list of books and a Series of Training Booklets. The address of the Council is 58, Queen Anne Street, W.1.

J. MacMurray, *Reason and Emotion* (Faber & Faber, 1962).

E. Thurneyson, *A Theology of Pastoral Care* (John Knox, 1962).

T. A. Ratcliffe, *The Development of Personality* (Allen & Unwin, 1967).

J. H. Kahn and G. M. Carstairs, *Human Growth* (Pergamon Publications, 1965).

J. MacMurray, *Persons in Relation* (Faber, 1935).

A. Storr, *The Integrity of the Personality* (Penguin Books)

H. Guntrip, *Personality Structure and Human Interaction* (Hogarth, 1961).

O. S. English and G. H. J. Pearson, *Emotional Problems of Living* (Allen & Unwin)

I. Suttie, *The Origins of Love and Hate* (Penguin Books)

H. Guntrip, *Psychology for Ministers and Social Workers* (Independent Press, 1949).

G. W. Allport, *Becoming* (Yale, 1955).

F. Lake, *Clinical Theology* (Darton, Longman & Todd, 1966).

J. H. Wallis, *Someone to turn to* (Routledge & Kegan Paul, 1962).

J. H. Wallis, *Counselling and Social Welfare* (Routledge, 1960).

L. Pincus, *Marriage* (Methuen, 1960).

Family Discussion Bureau, *The Marital Relationship as a Focus for Casework*

M. L. Ferard and N. K. Hunnybun, *The Caseworker's Use of Relationships* (Tavistock)

C. A. Wise, *Pastoral Counselling* (Harper & Row)

J. Wallis, *Sexual Harmony in Marriage* (Routledge, 1964).

M. Macaulay, *The Art of Marriage* (Delisle, 1956).

M. Davis, *Sexual Responsibility in Marriage* (Fontana)
H. Wright, *The Sex Factor in Marriage* (Benn)
P. M. Bloom, *Modern Contraception* (Delisle, 1964).
J. Wallis, *Thinking About Marriage* (Penguin)
E. F. Griffith, *Modern Marriage* (Methuen, 1963).
T. H. Van de Velde, *Ideal Marriage* (Heinemann)
J. Malleson, *Any Wife or Any Husband* (Heinemann)
E. Fromm, *The Art of Loving* (Allen & Unwin, 1957).
A. Storr, *Sexual Deviation* (Penguin Books)
W. Stekel, *Frigidity in Women* (Vision, 1960).
L. Friedman, *Virgin Wives* (Tavistock, 1962).
Kinsey, Pomeroy, and Martin, *Sexual Behavior in the Human Male* (W. B. Saunders, 1948).
Kinsey, Pomeroy, Martin, and Gebhard, *Sexual Behavior in the Human Female* (W. B. Saunders, 1948).

P. Halmos, *The Faith of the Counsellors* (Constable, 1965).
R. Haughton, *The Transformation of Man* (Geoffrey Chapman, 1967).
L. Hodgson, *Sex and Christian Freedom* (S.C.M., 1967).
M. Thurian, *Marriage and Celibacy* (S.C.M., 1959).
Putting Asunder (S.P.C.K., 1966).

Index